FOR ORGANS, PIANOS & ELECTRONIC KEYBOARDS

E•Z PLAY® TODAY

370

MORE SONGS OF THE FIFTIES

THE DECADE

ISBN 0-7935-3101-2

HAL•LEONARD®
CORPORATION
7777 W. BLUEMOUND RD. P.O. BOX 13819 MILWAUKEE, WI 53213

E-Z Play ® Today Music Notation © 1975 by HAL LEONARD CORPORATION
E-Z PLAY and EASY ELECTRONIC KEYBOARD MUSIC are registered trademarks of HAL LEONARD CORPORATION

CONTENTS

All The Way
(From "THE JOKER IS WILD")

Registration 3
Rhythm: Fox Trot or Ballad

Words by Sammy Cahn
Music by James Van Heusen

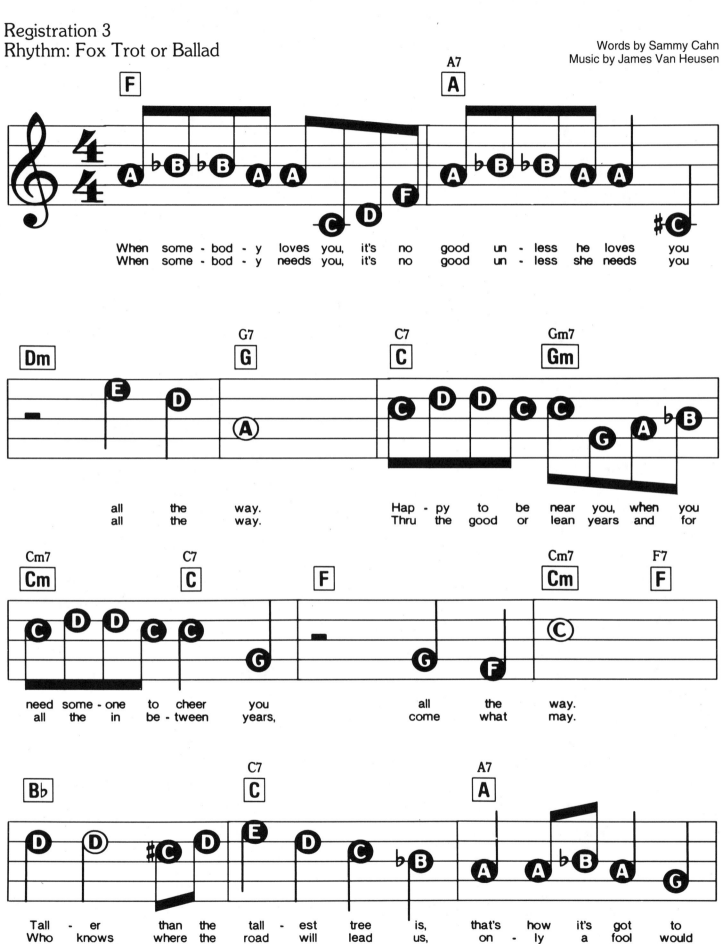

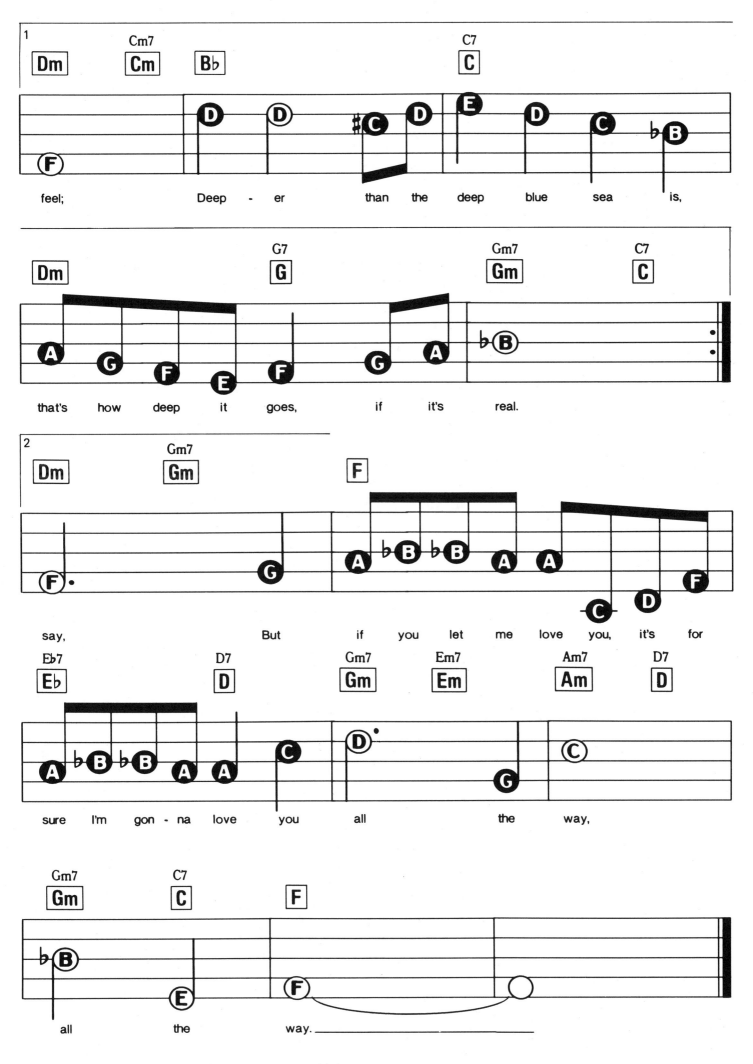

Allegheny Moon

Registration 9
Rhythm: Waltz

Words and Music by
Al Hoffman and Dick Manning

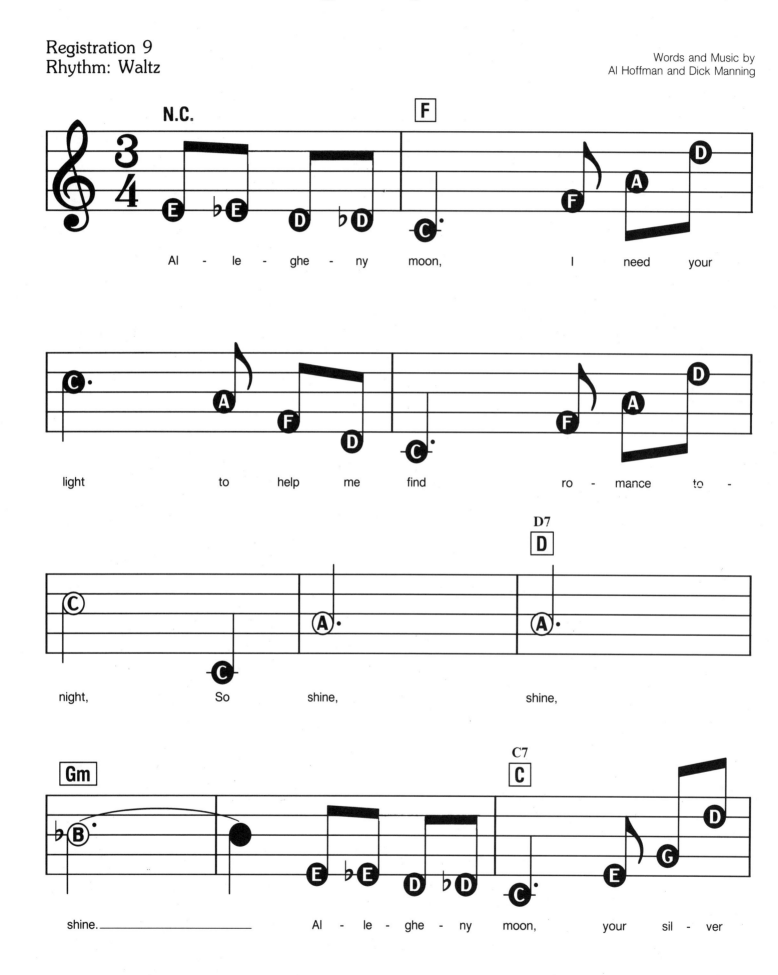

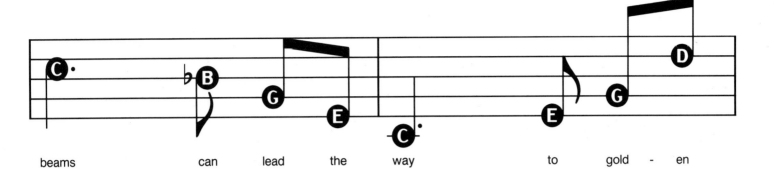

beams   can   lead   the   way   to   gold - en

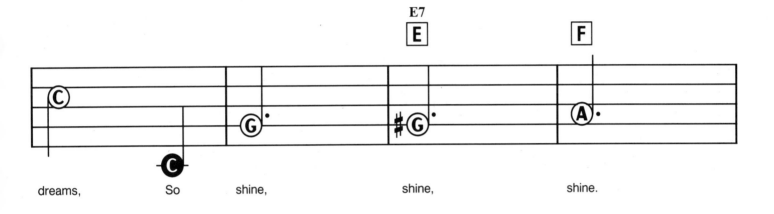

dreams,   So   shine,   shine,   shine.

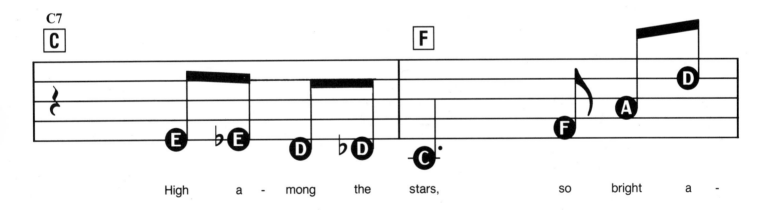

High   a - mong   the   stars,   so   bright a -

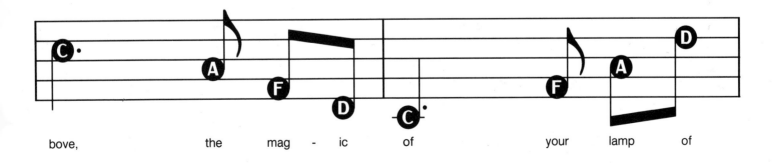

bove,   the mag - ic   of   your   lamp   of

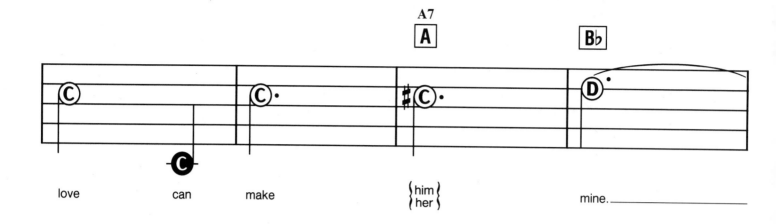

love can make {him her} mine.____

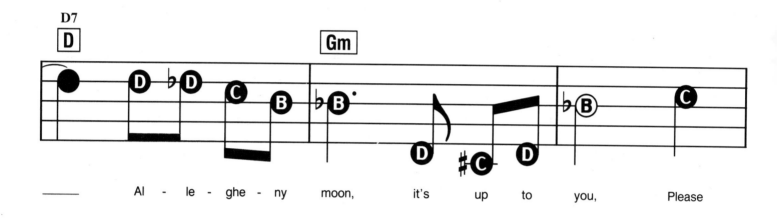

____ Al - le - ghe - ny moon, it's up to you, Please

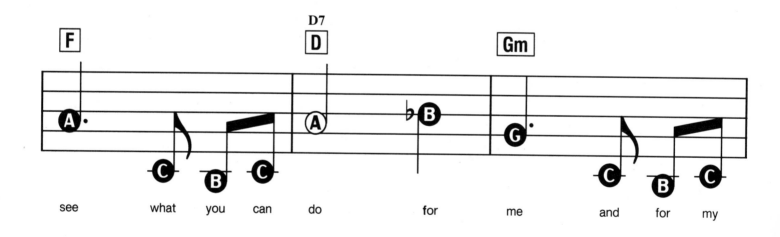

see what you can do for me and for my

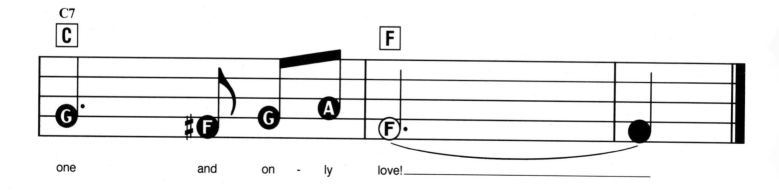

one and on - ly love!____

Alright, Okay, You Win

Registration 7
Rhythm: Swing

Words and Music by Sid Wyche
and Mayme Watts

Well, al - right, o - kay, you win, I'm in love with you. Well, al - right, o - kay, you win, Ba - by, what can I do? I'll do an - y - thing you say, It's just got - ta be that way. Well, al - right, o - kay, you win I'm in love with you. Well, al - right, o -

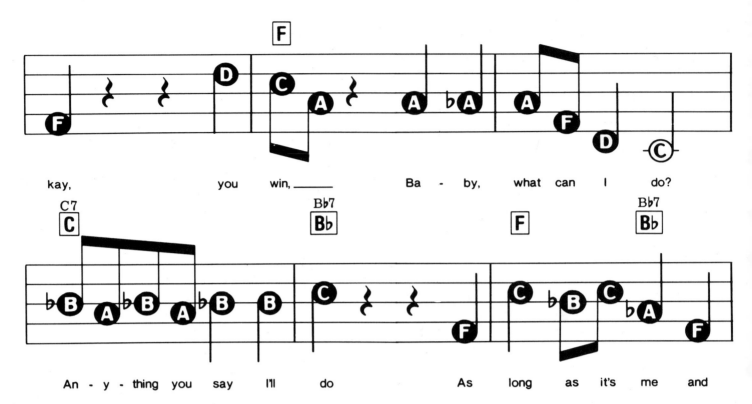

kay,   you win, _____ Ba - by, what can I do?

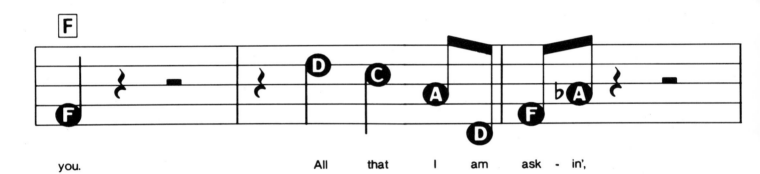

An - y - thing you say I'll do   As long as it's me and

you.   All that I am ask - in',

All I want from you,   Just love me like

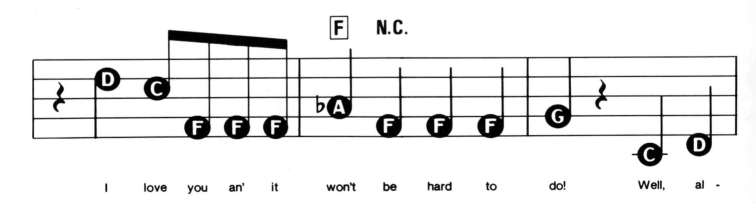

I love you an' it won't be hard to do!   Well, al -

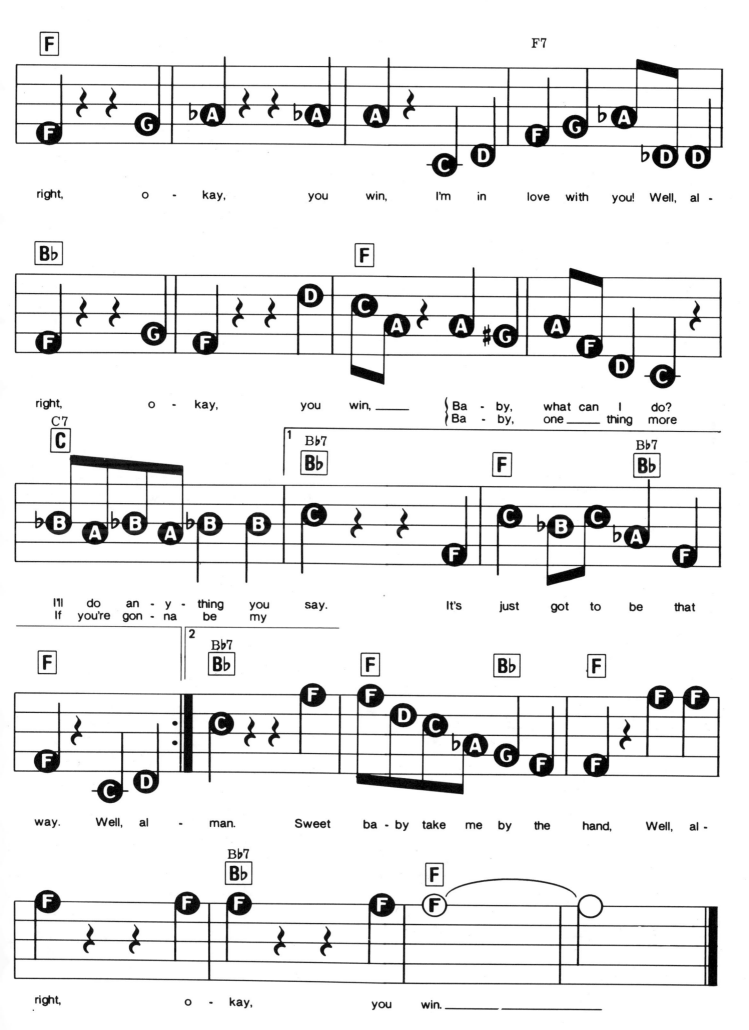

Baby
(You've Got What It Takes)

Registration 5
Rhythm: Shuffle or Swing

Words and Music by Clyde Otis
and Murray Stein

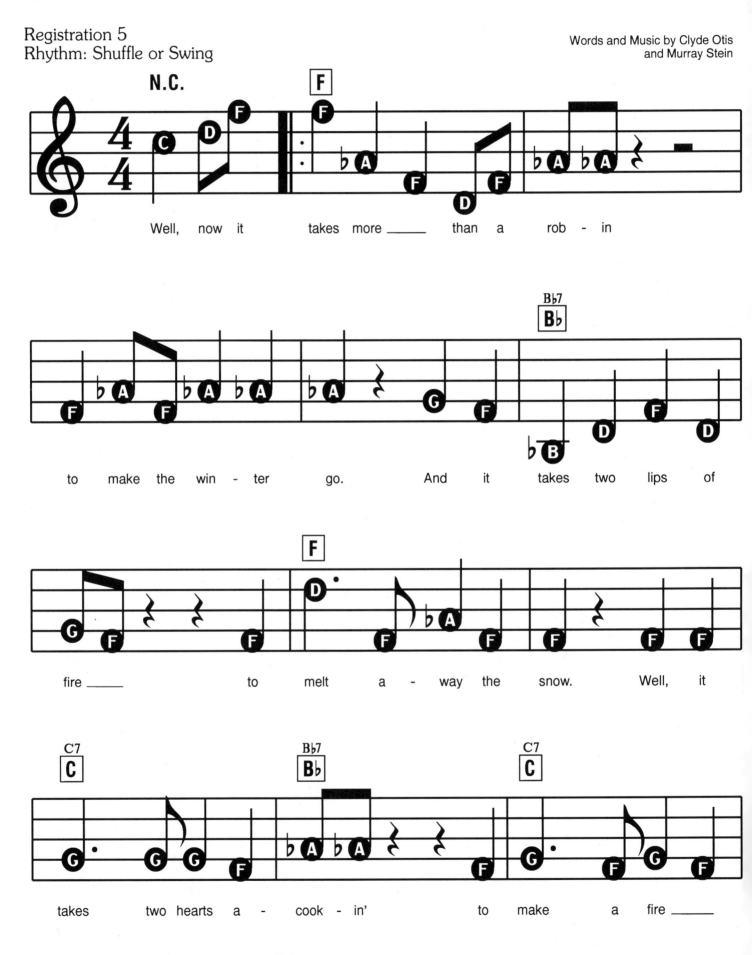

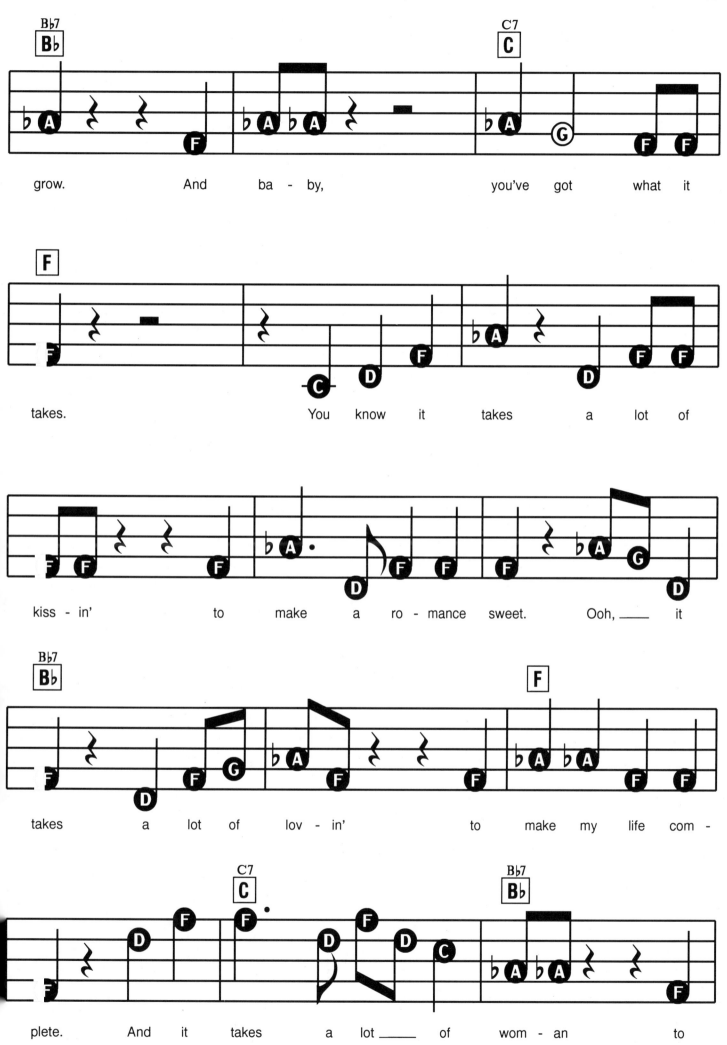

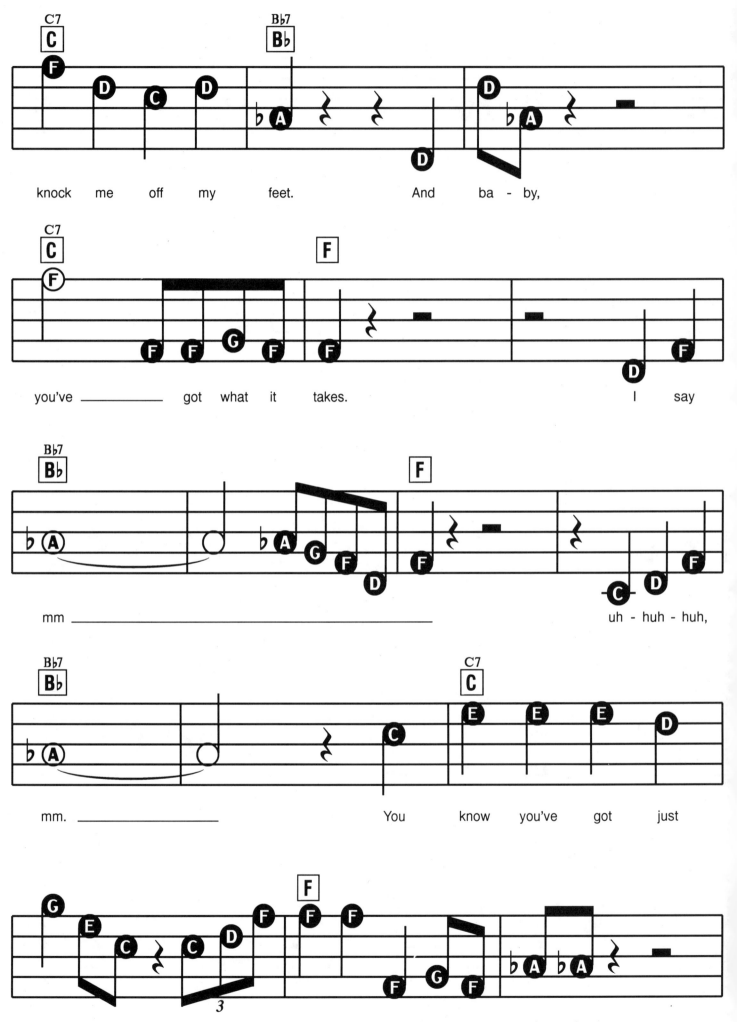

The Sound of Music
from THE SOUND OF MUSIC

Registration 5
Rhythm: Fox Trot

Lyrics by Oscar Hammerstein II
Music by Richard Rodgers

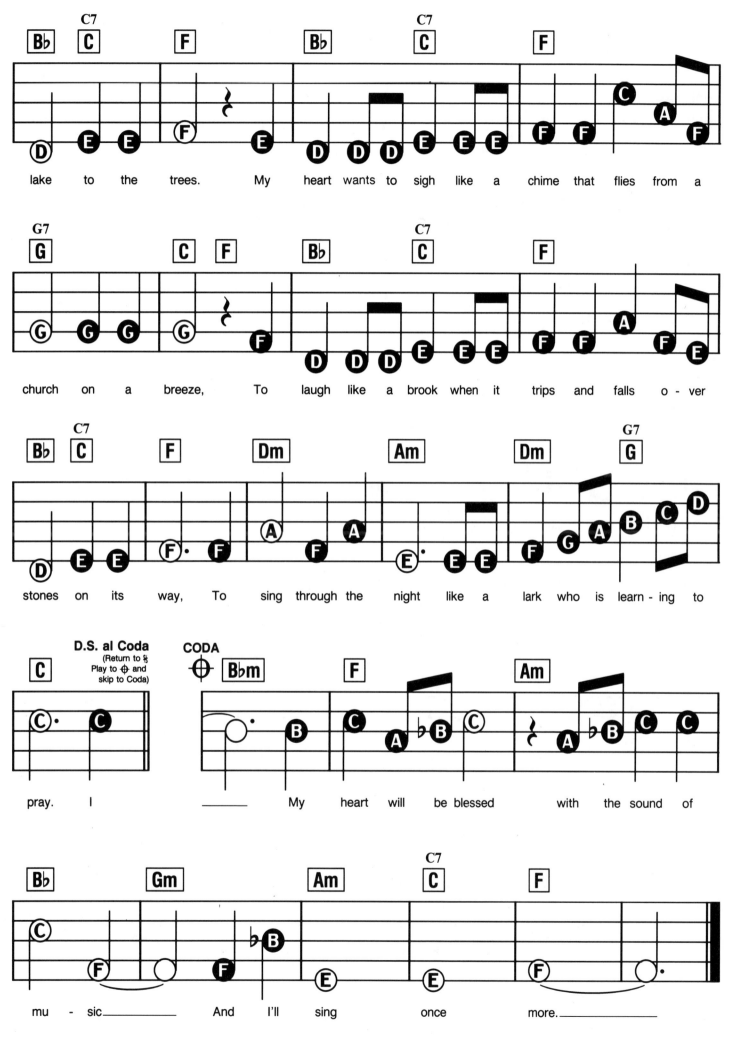

The Bible Tells Me So

Registration 6
Rhythm: 8-Beat, Pops or March

Words and Music by
Dale Evans

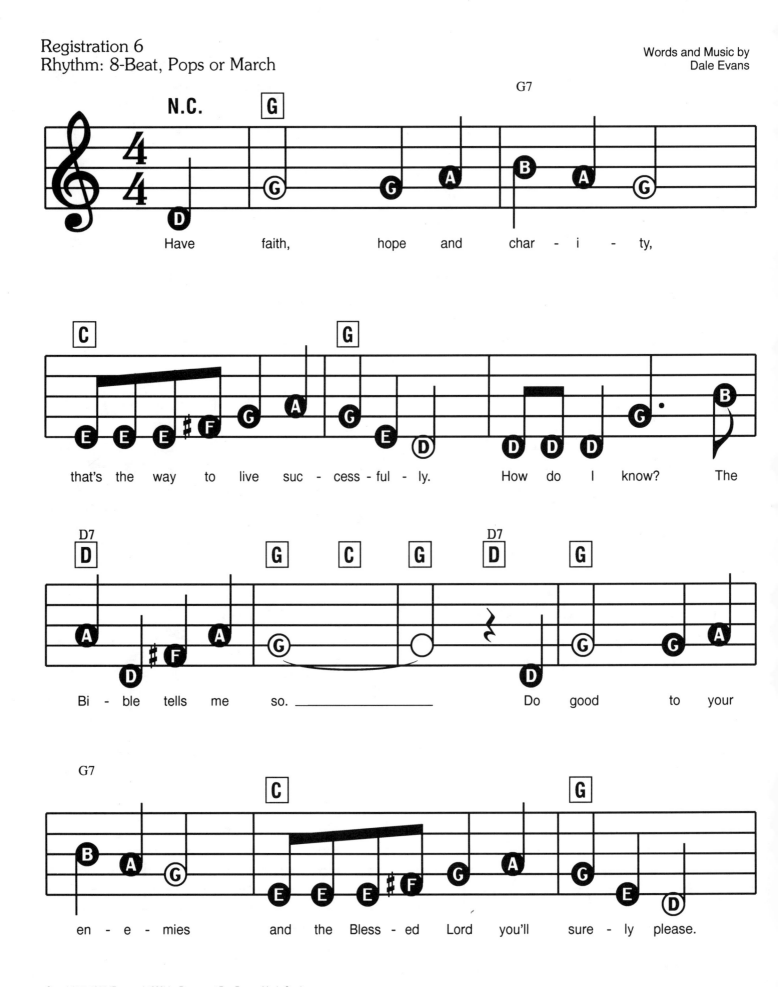

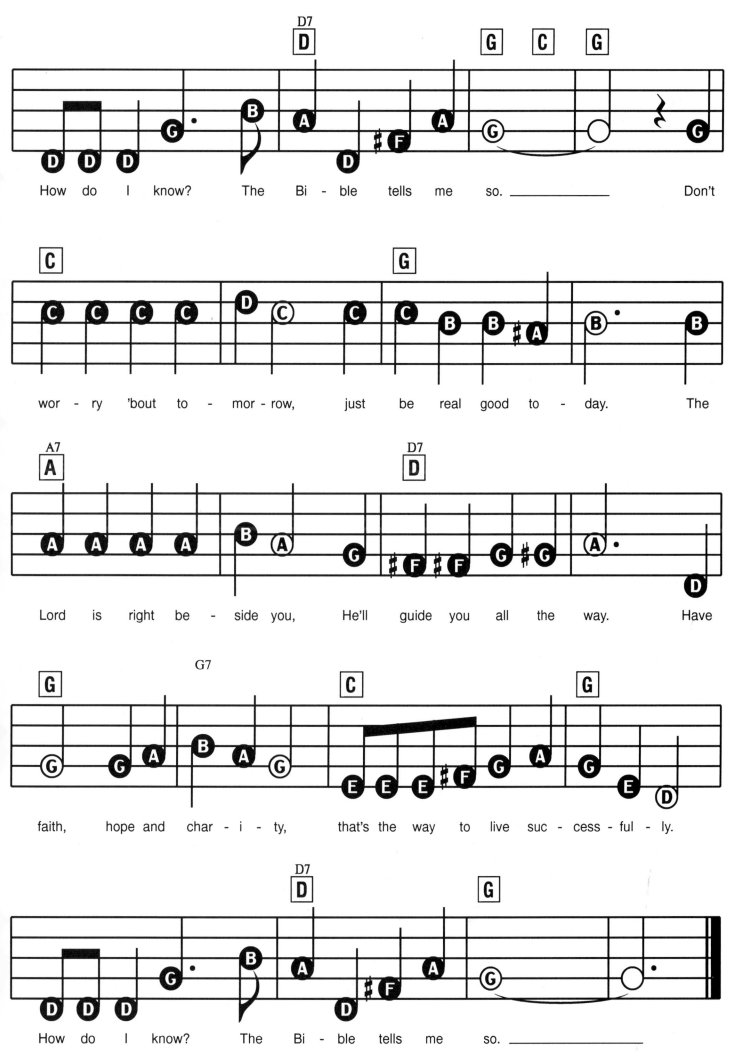

Blueberry Hill

Registration 2
Rhythm: Fox Trot or Swing

Words and Music by Al Lewis,
Larry Stock and Vincent Rose

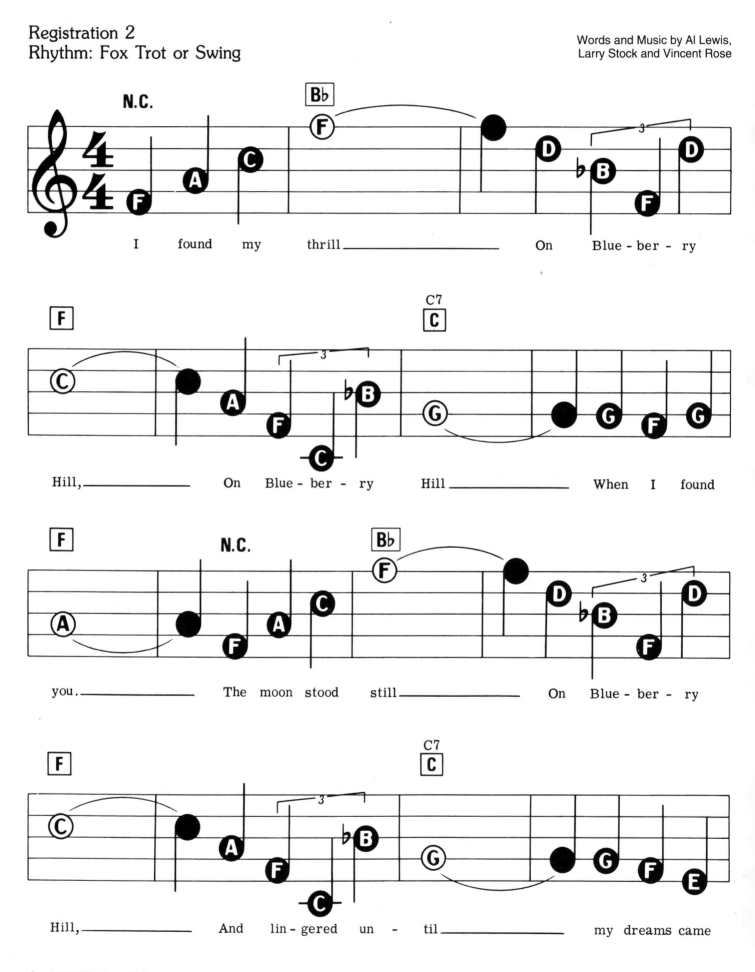

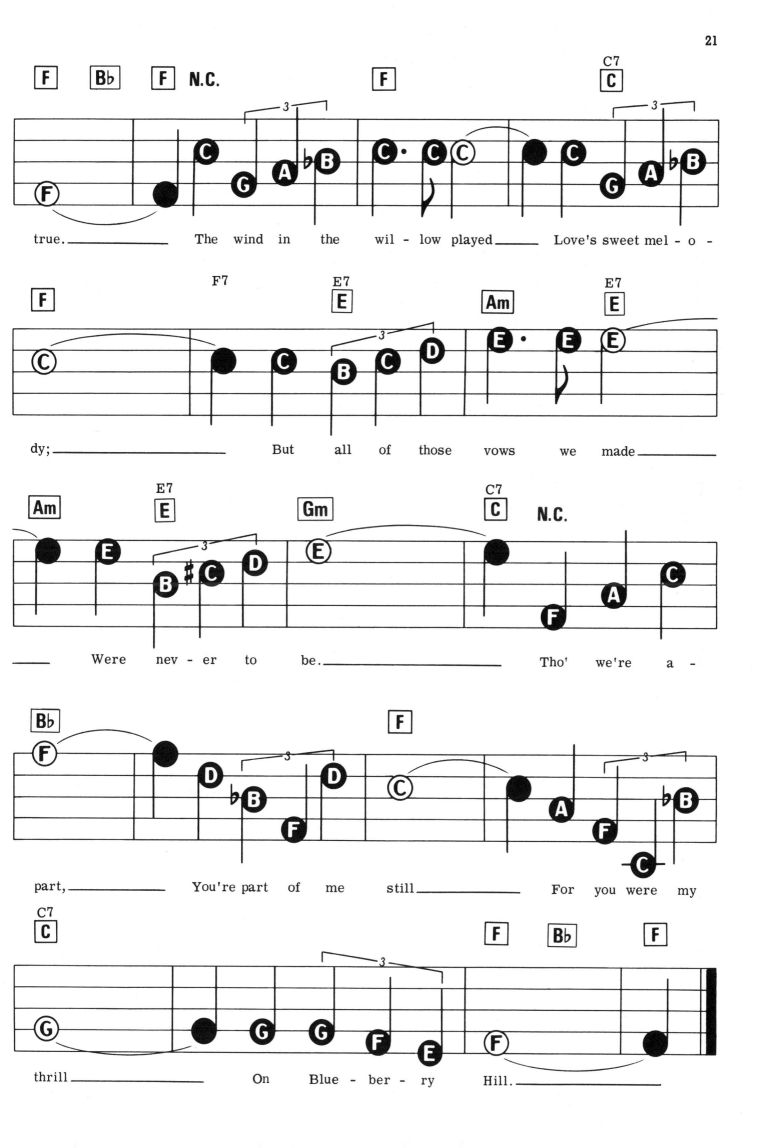

Where Is Your Heart
(The Song from Moulin Rouge)
from MOULIN ROUGE

Registration 2
Rhythm: Waltz

Words by William Engvick
Music by George Auric

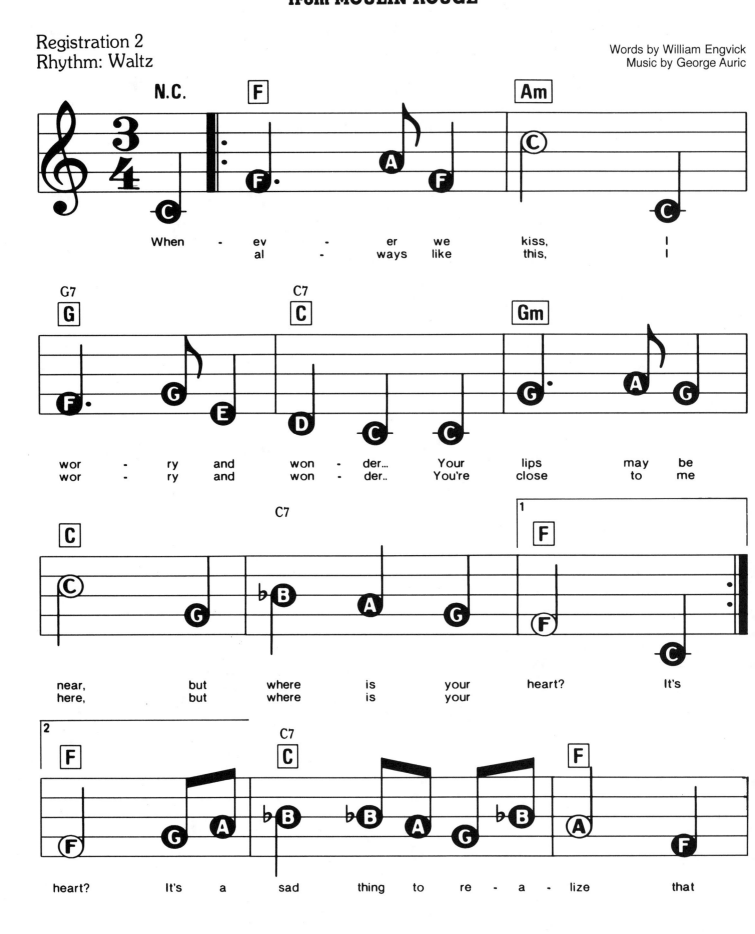

Bird Dog

Registration 7
Rhythm: Rock or 8-Beat

By Boudleaux Bryant

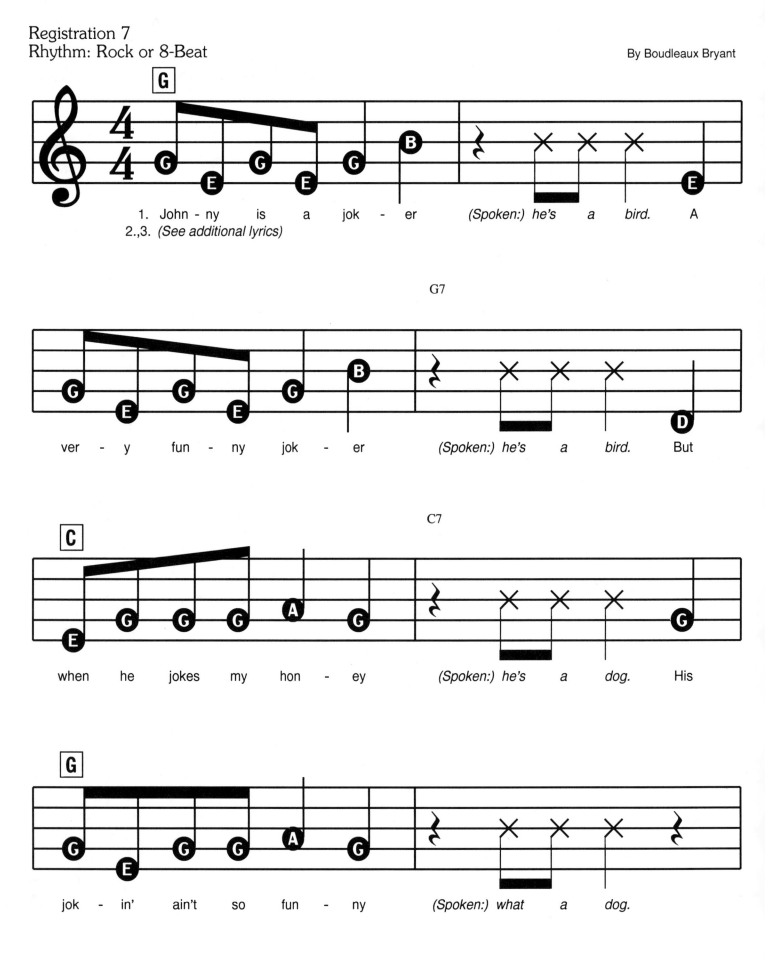

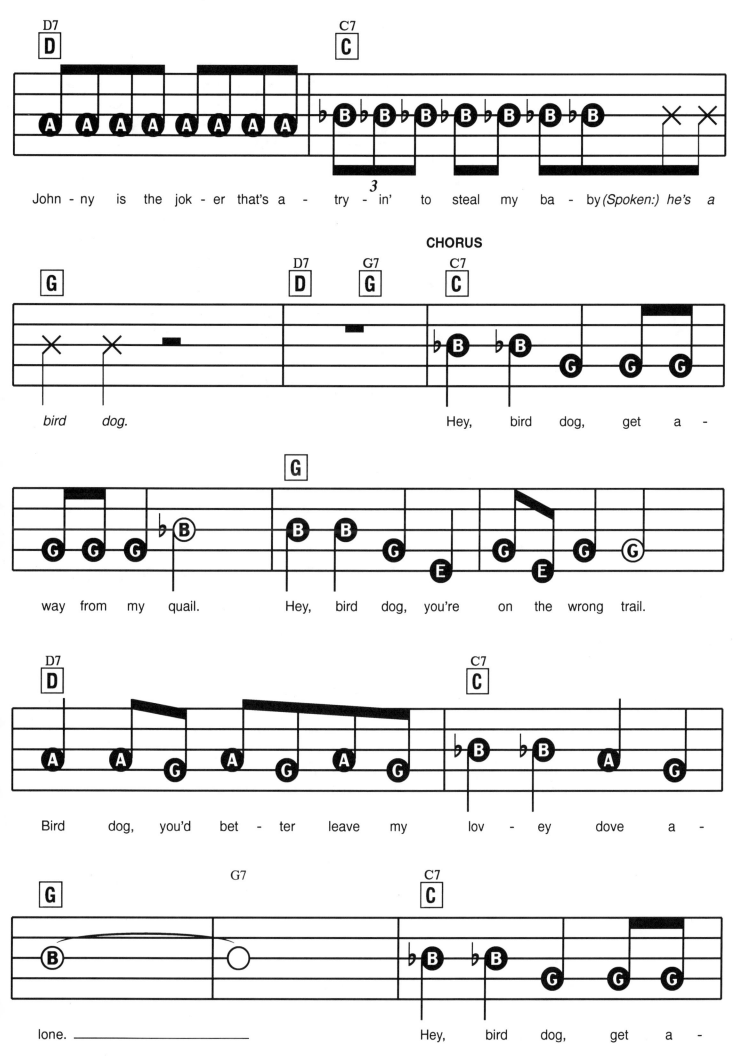

John - ny   is   the   jok - er   that's   a - try - in'   to   steal   my   ba - by *(Spoken:) he's a*

CHORUS

bird   dog.   Hey,   bird   dog,   get   a -

way   from   my   quail.   Hey,   bird   dog,   you're   on   the   wrong   trail.

Bird   dog,   you'd   bet - ter   leave   my   lov - ey   dove   a -

lone. _____   Hey,   bird   dog,   get   a -

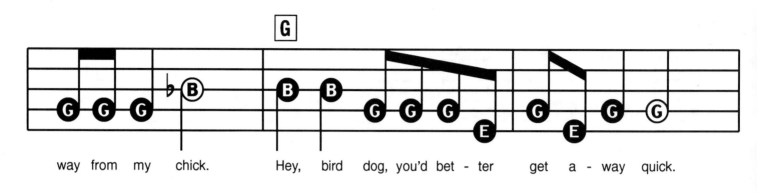

way from my chick. Hey, bird dog, you'd bet - ter get a - way quick.

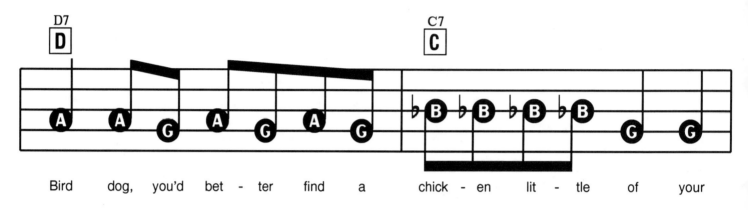

Bird dog, you'd bet - ter find a chick - en lit - tle of your

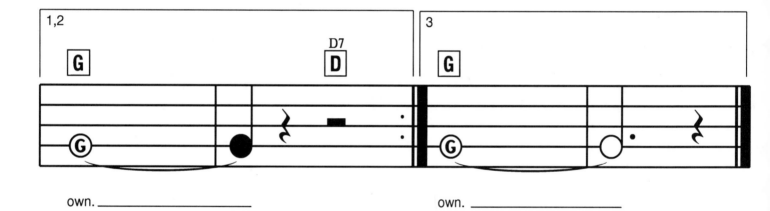

own. _____ own. _____

Additional Lyrics

2. Johnny sings a love song *(Like a bird)*
   He sings the sweetest love song *(You ever heard)*
   But when he sings to my gal *(What a howl)*
   To me he's just a wolf dog *(On the prowl)*
   Johnny wants to fly away and puppy love my baby *(He's a bird dog)*
   To Chorus

3. Johnny kissed the teacher *(He's a bird)*
   He tiptoed up to reach her *(He's a bird)*
   Well, he's the teacher's pet now *(He's a dog)*
   What he wants he can get now *(What a dog)*
   He even made the teacher let him sit next to my baby. *(He's a bird dog)*
   To Chorus

Happy, Happy Birthday Baby

Registration 6
Rhythm: Rock or Shuffle

Words and Music by Margo Sylvia
and Gilbert Lopez

ba - by.
Instrumental

No, I can't call you my ba - by.

Seems like years a - go we met on a day I can't for -

get, 'cause that's when we fell in love. *Instrumental ends* Do you re -

mem - ber the names we had for each oth - er?

You were my pret - ty, I was your ba - by.

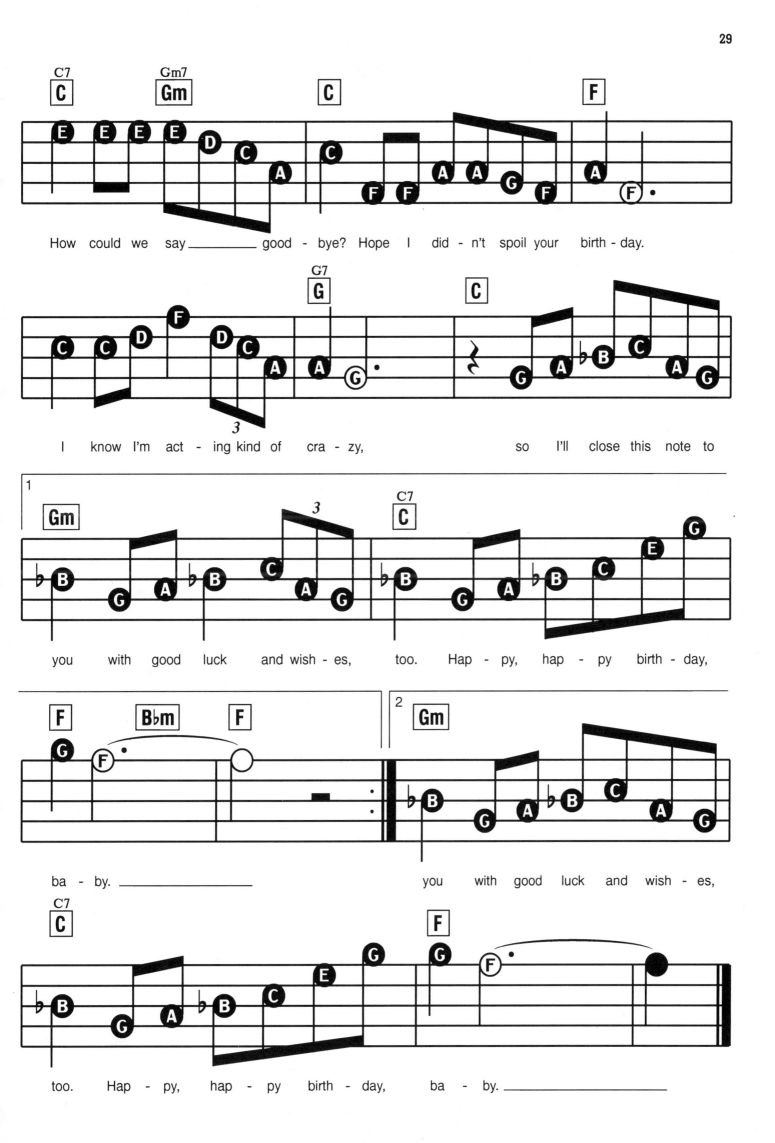

Chanson D'Amour
(The Ra-Da-Da-Da-Da Song)

Registration 7
Rhythm: Swing or Jazz

Words and Music by
Wayne Shanklin

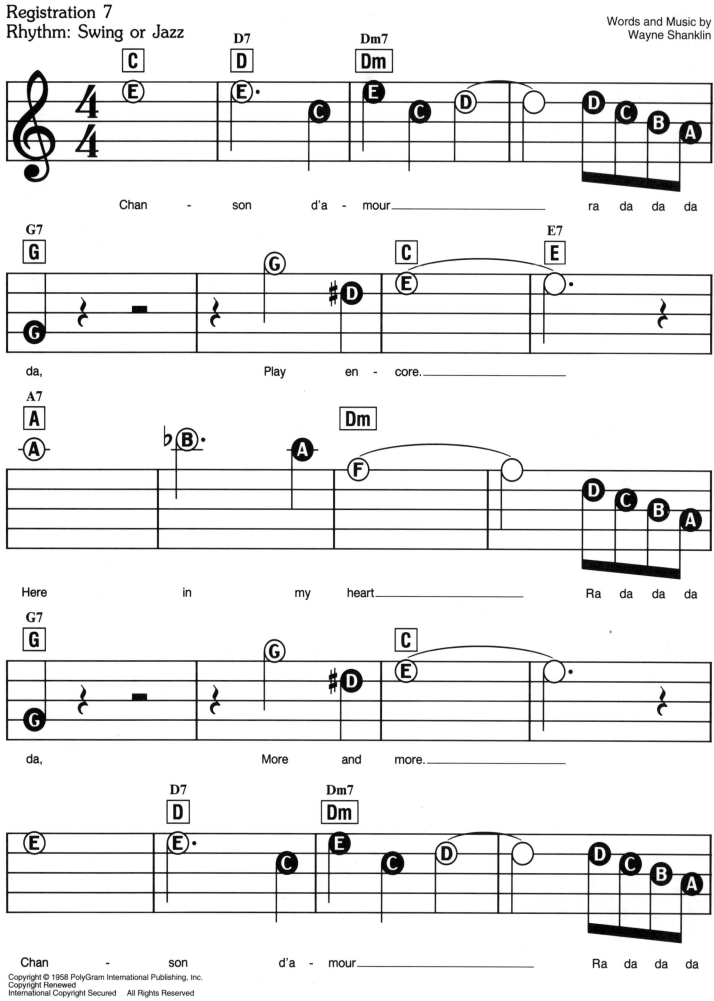

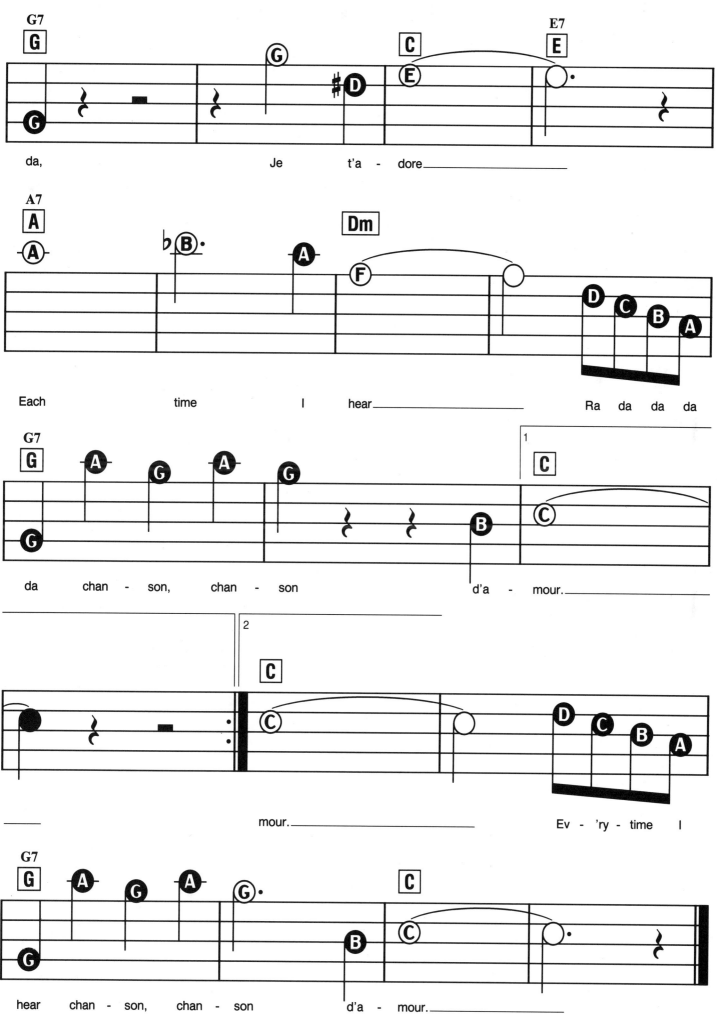

da,   Je   t'a - dore_____

Each   time   I   hear_____   Ra   da   da   da

da   chan - son,   chan - son   d'a - mour._____

___   mour._____   Ev - 'ry - time   I

hear chan - son,   chan - son   d'a - mour._____

Charlie Brown

Registration 2
Rhythm: Rock

Words and Music by Jerry Leiber
and Mike Stoller

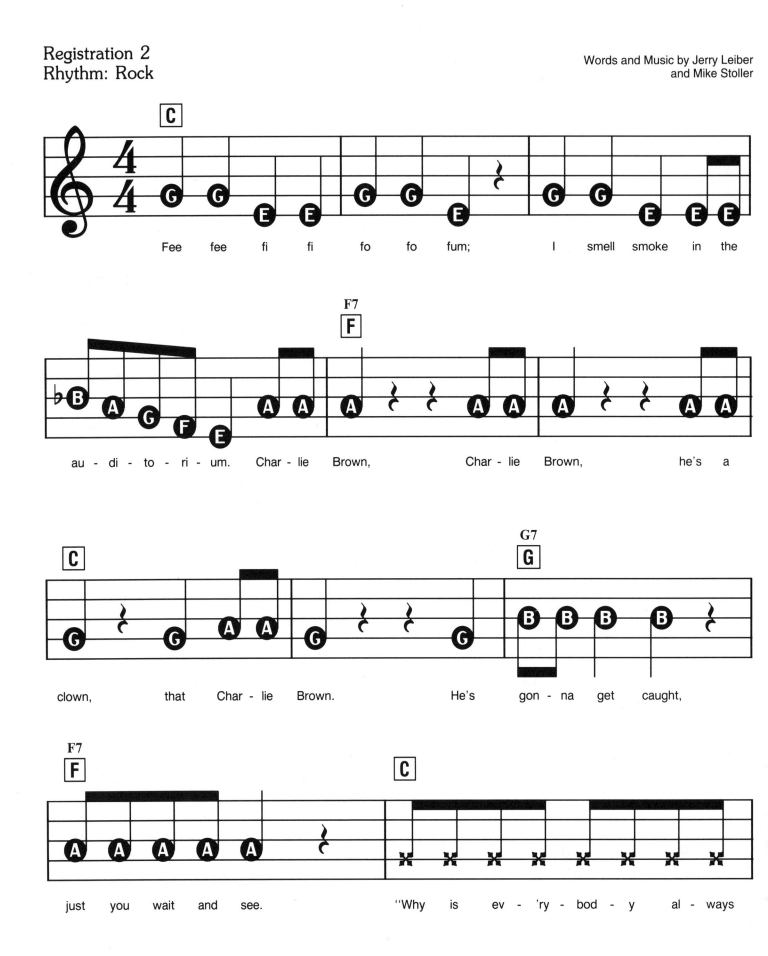

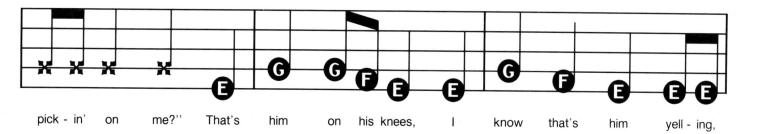

pick - in' on me?" That's him on his knees, I know that's him yell - ing,

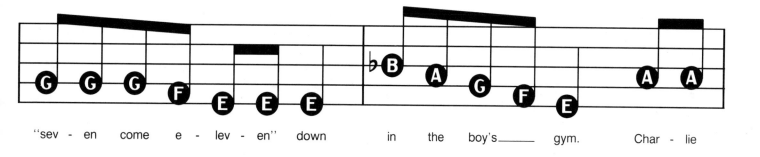

"sev - en come e - lev - en" down in the boy's_____ gym. Char - lie

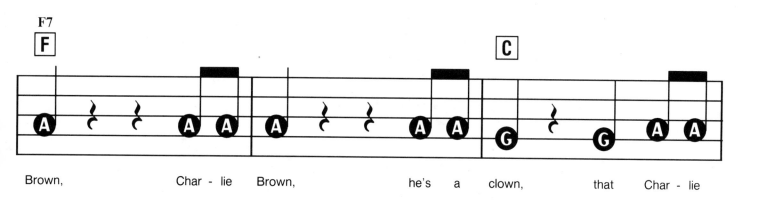

Brown, Char - lie Brown, he's a clown, that Char - lie

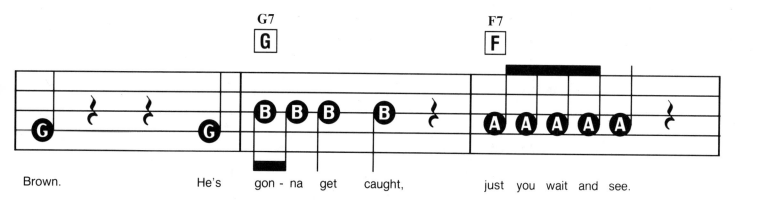

Brown. He's gon - na get caught, just you wait and see.

34

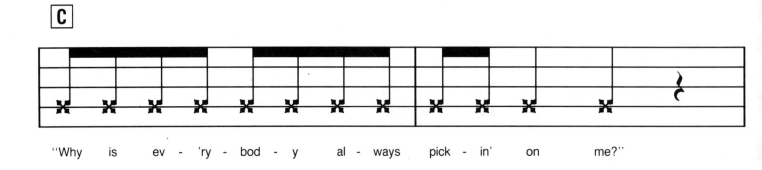

C

"Why is ev - 'ry - bod - y al - ways pick - in' on me?"

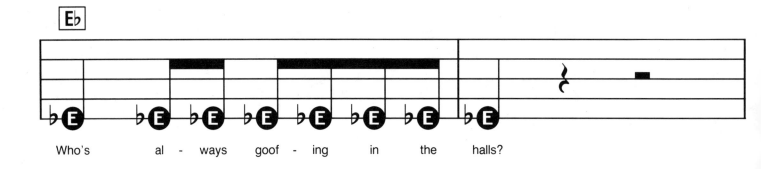

F

Who's al - ways writ - ing on the walls?

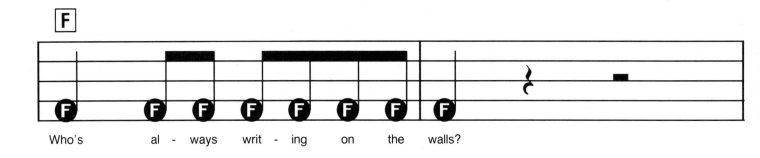

E♭

Who's al - ways goof - ing in the halls?

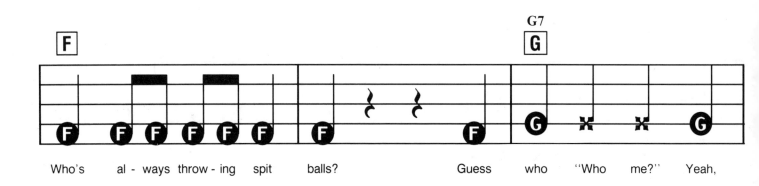

F
G7
G

Who's al - ways throw - ing spit balls?   Guess who "Who me?" Yeah,

35

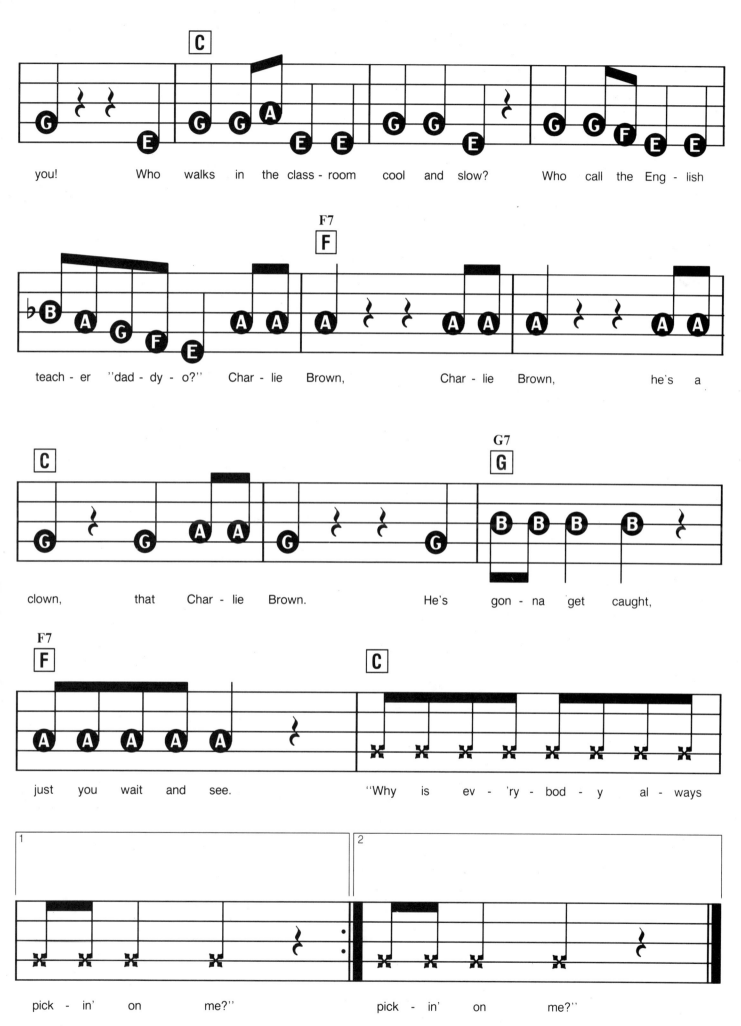

The Chipmunk Song

Registration 3
Rhythm: Waltz

Words and Music by
Ross Bagdasarian

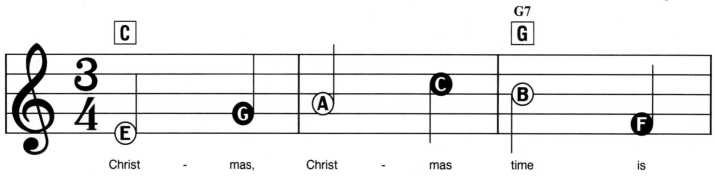

Christ - mas, Christ - mas time is

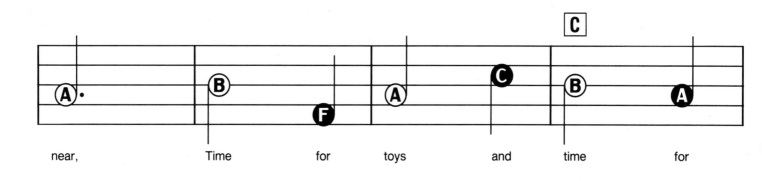

near, Time for toys and time for

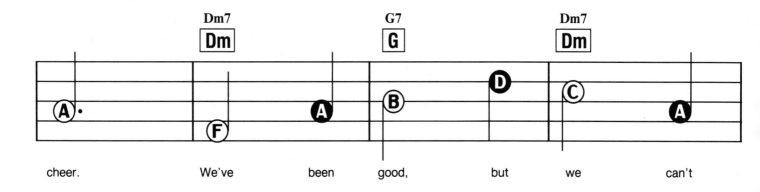

cheer. We've been good, but we can't

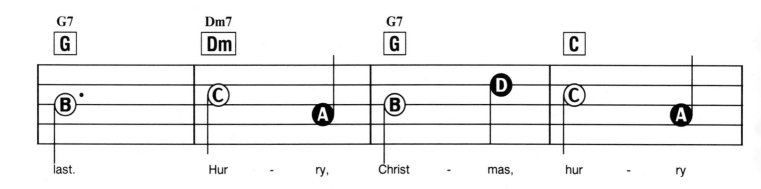

last. Hur - ry, Christ - mas, hur - ry

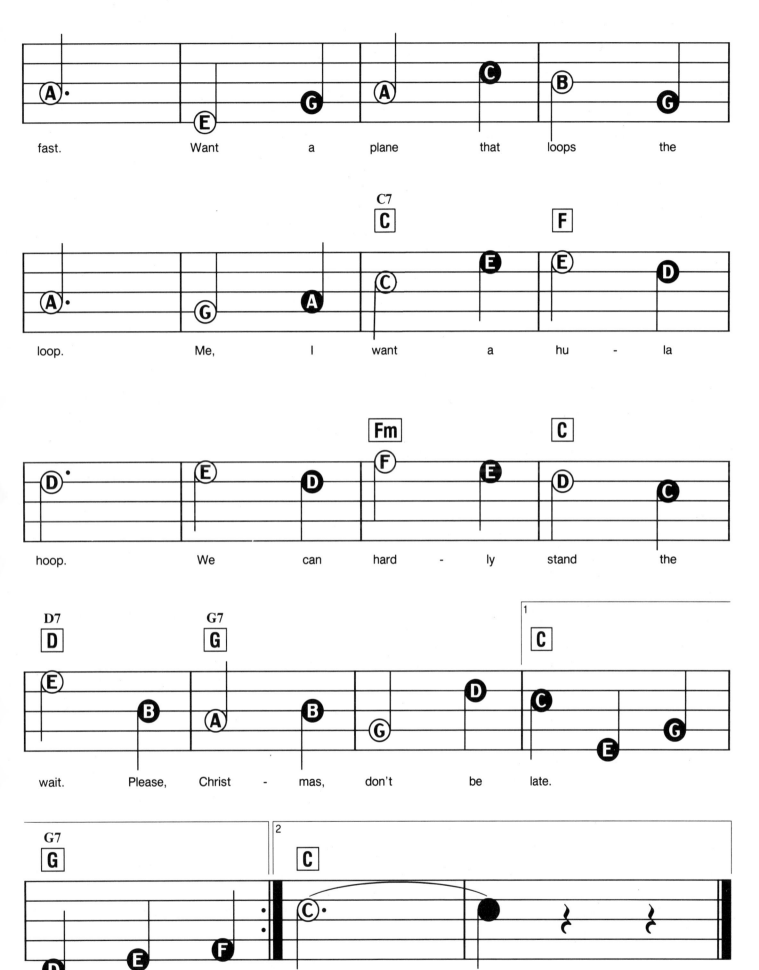

Do I Love You Because You're Beautiful?

(From "CINDERELLA")

Registration 2
Rhythm: Fox Trot or Swing

Lyrics by Oscar Hammerstein II
Music by Richard Rodgers

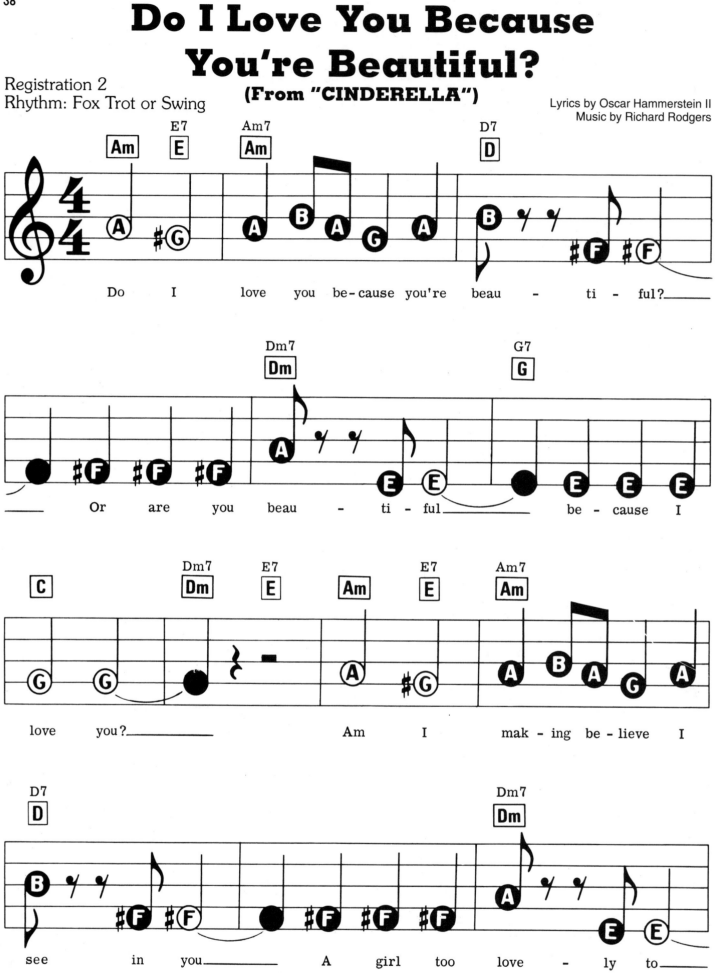

Do I love you be-cause you're beau - ti - ful?_____

_____ Or are you beau - ti - ful_____ be - cause I

love you?_____ Am I mak - ing be - lieve I

see in you_____ A girl too love - ly to_____

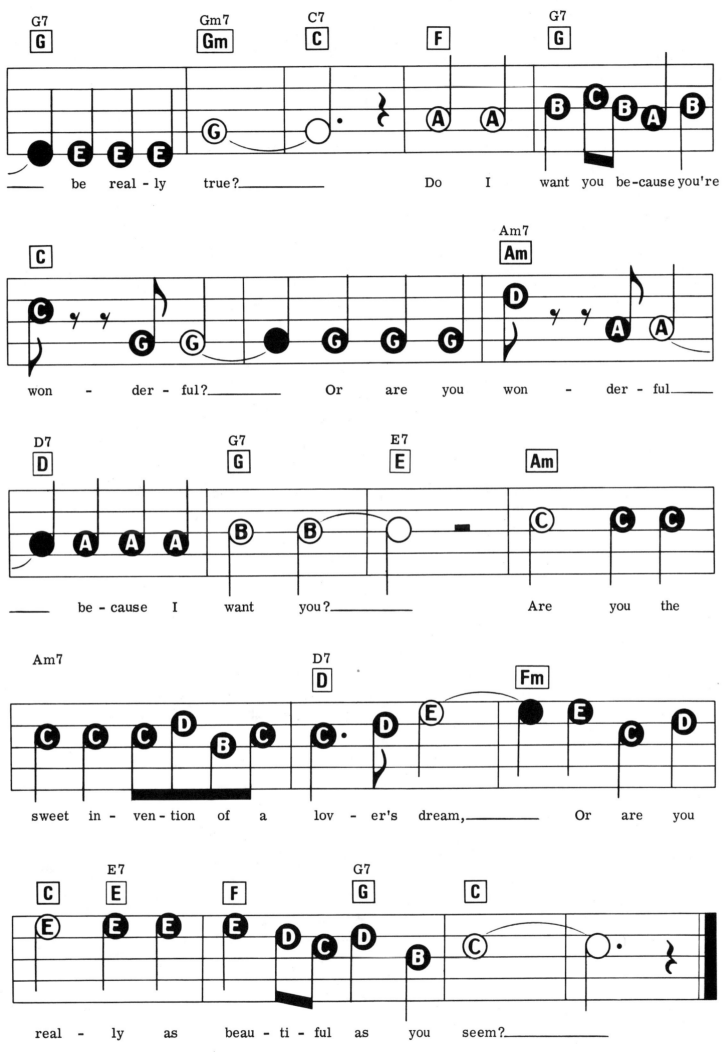

Do-Re-Mi
(From "THE SOUND OF MUSIC")

Registration 4
Rhythm: March

Lyrics by Oscar Hammerstein II
Music by Richard Rodgers

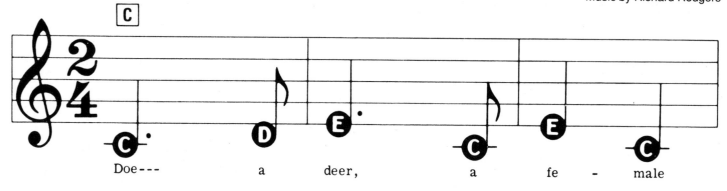

Doe--- a deer, a fe - male

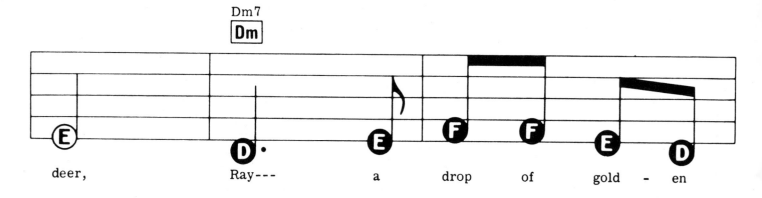

deer, Ray--- a drop of gold - en

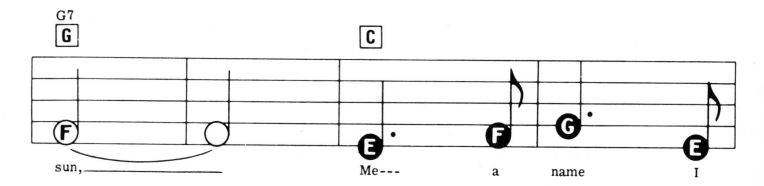

sun,_____ Me--- a name I

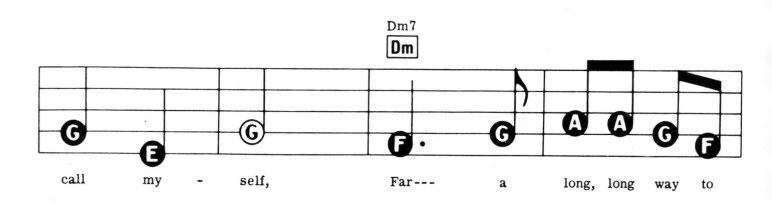

call my - self, Far--- a long, long way to

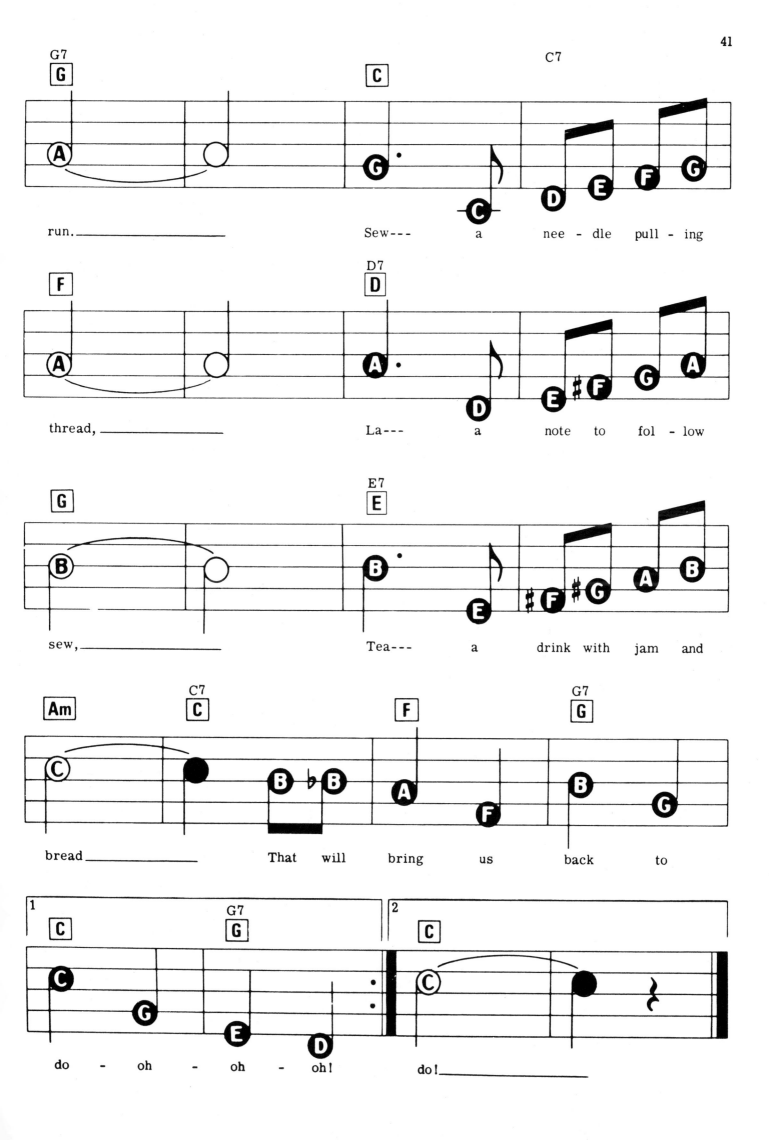

Domino

English Words by Don Raye
French Words by Jacques Plante
Music by Louis Ferrari

Registration 10
Rhythm: Waltz

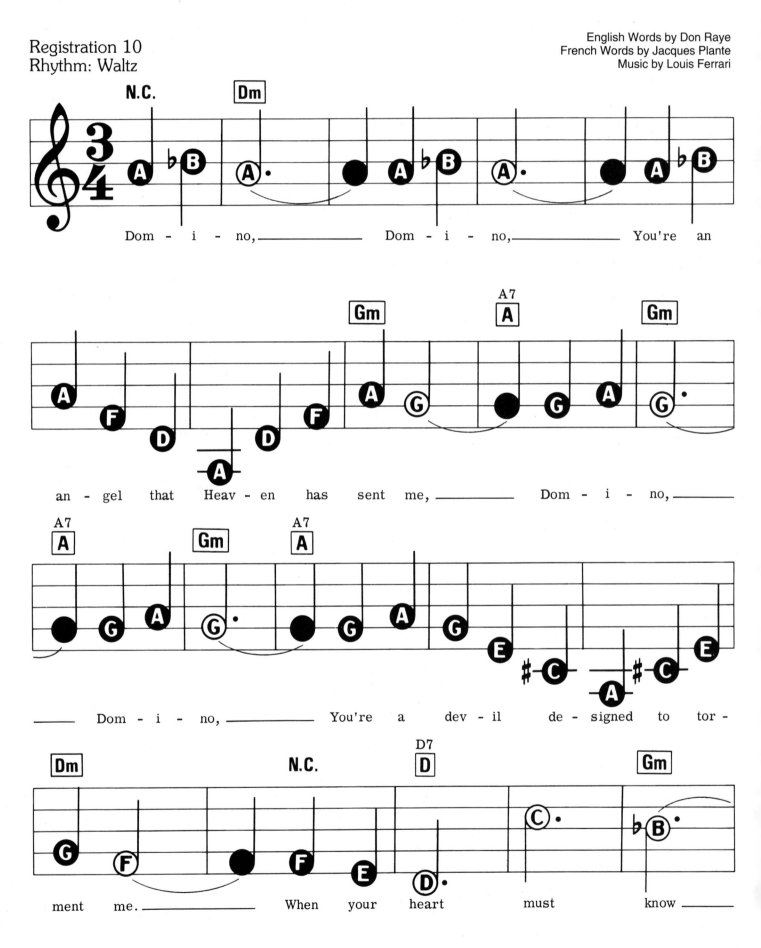

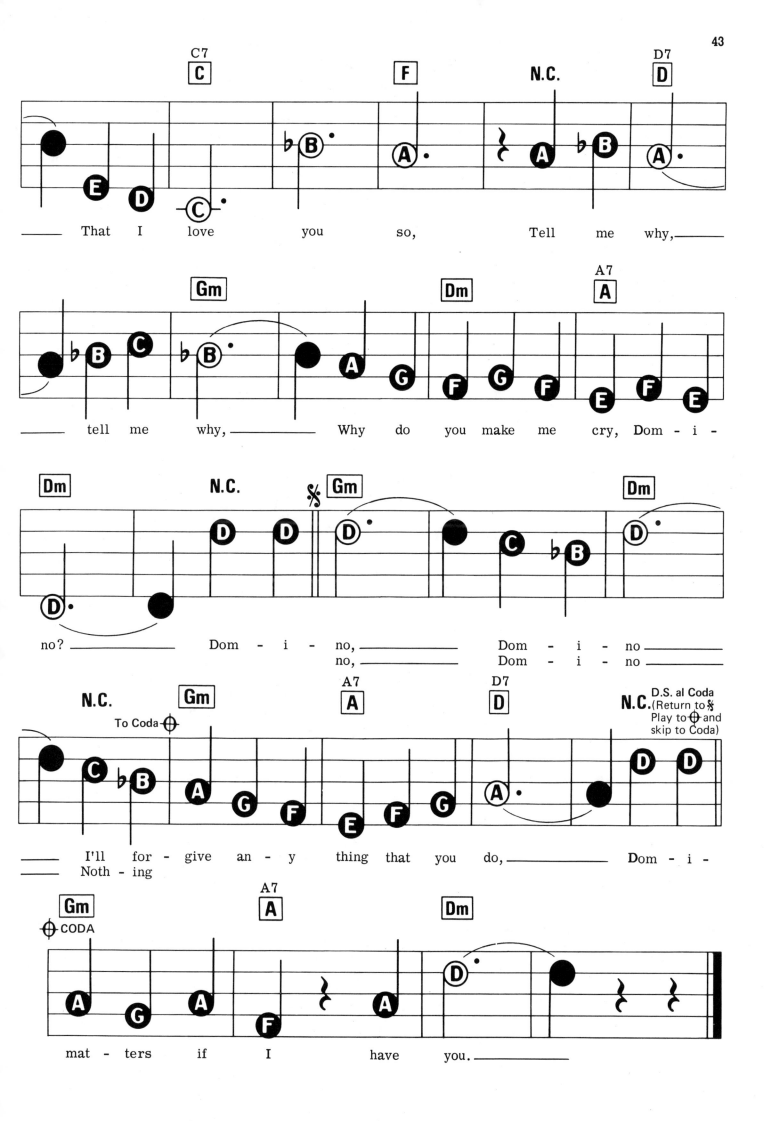

Fly Me To The Moon
(In Other Words)

Registration 2
Rhythm: Waltz or Jazz Waltz

Words and Music by
Bart Howard

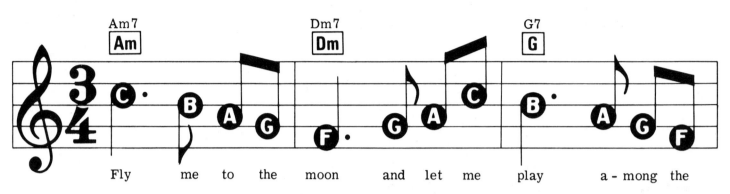

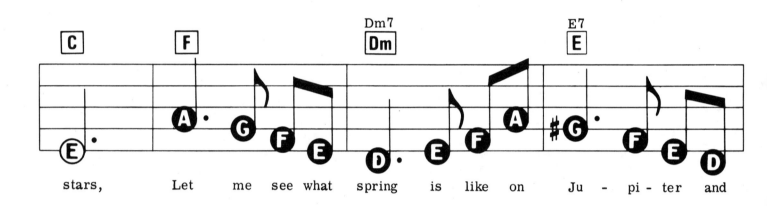

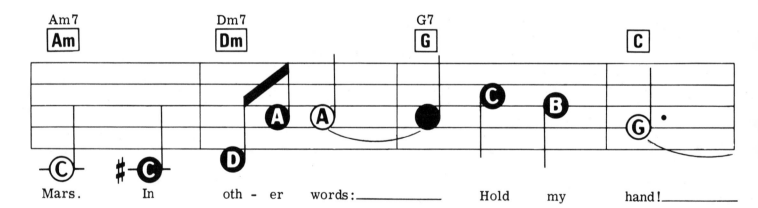

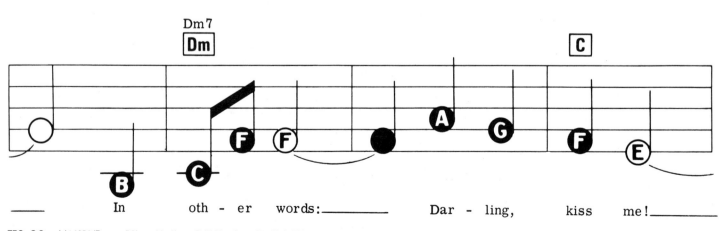

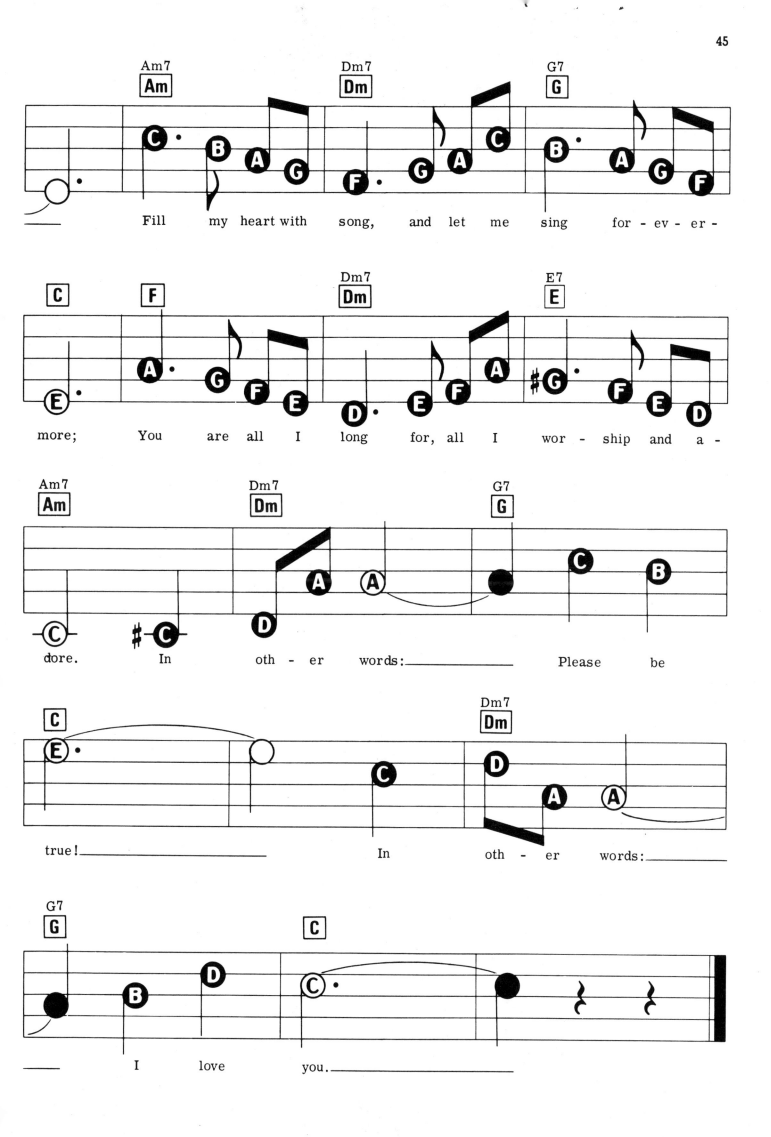

From This Moment On
(From "OUT OF THIS WORLD")

Registration 5
Rhythm: Swing

Words and Music by
Cole Porter

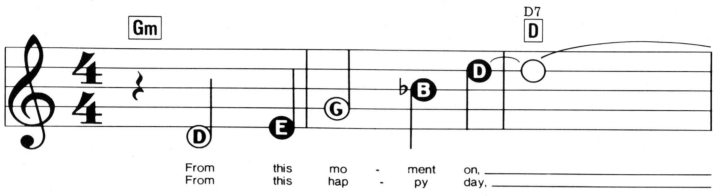

From this mo - ment on, _____
From this hap - py day, _____

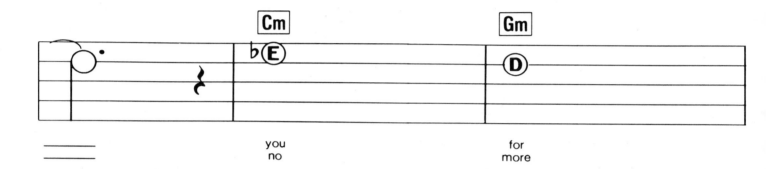

_____ you for
_____ no more

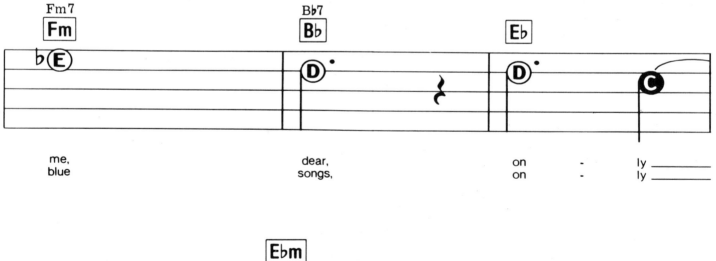

me, dear, on - ly _____
blue songs, on - ly _____

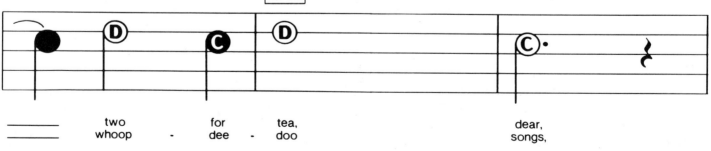

_____ two for tea, dear,
whoop - dee - doo songs,

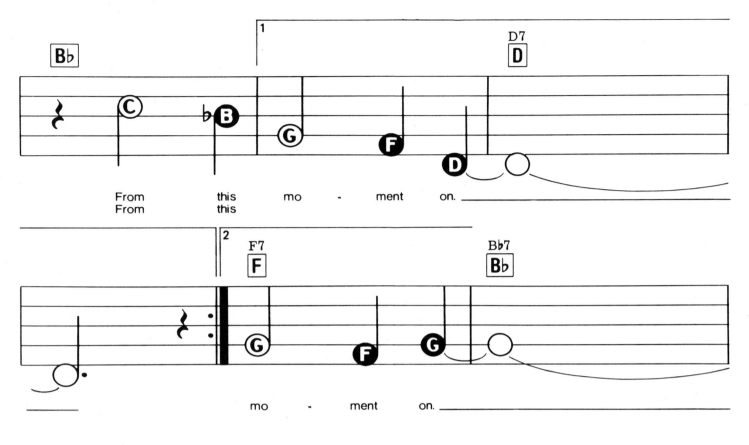

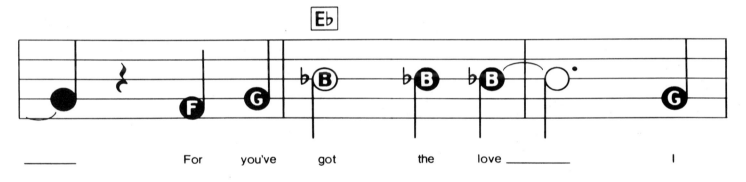

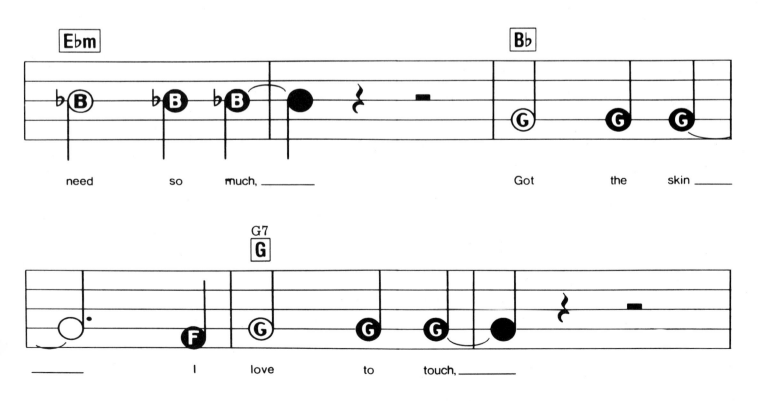

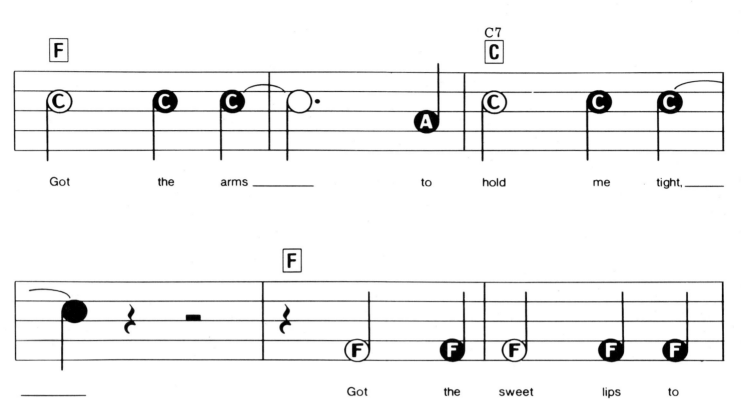

Got the arms _____ to hold me tight, _____

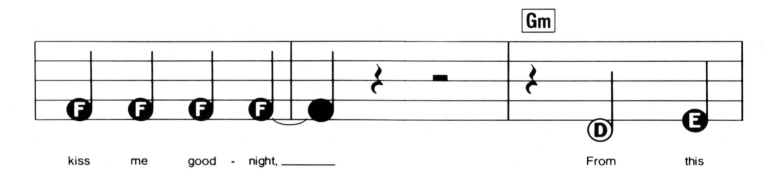

_____ Got the sweet lips to

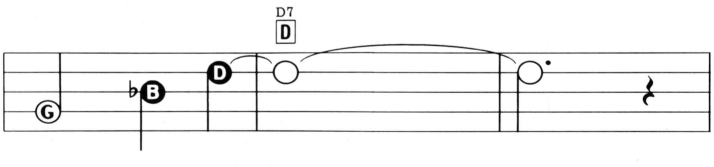

kiss me good - night, _____ From this

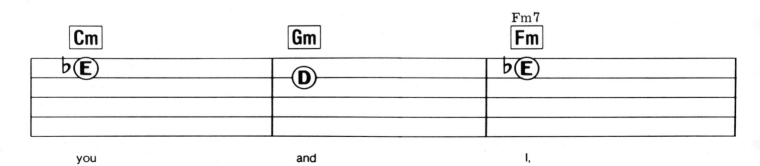

mo - ment on, _____

you and I,

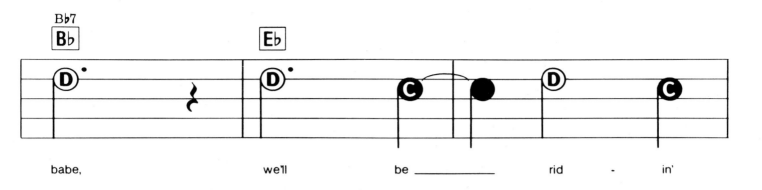

babe,   we'll   be _____ rid - in'

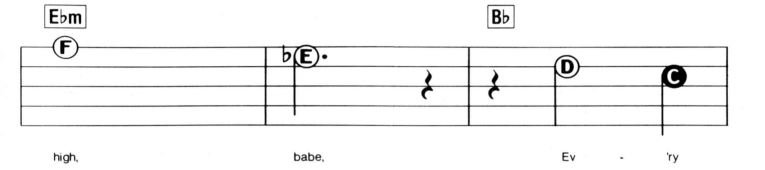

high,   babe,   Ev - 'ry

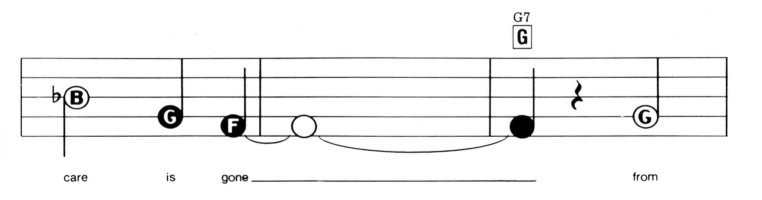

care   is   gone _____ from

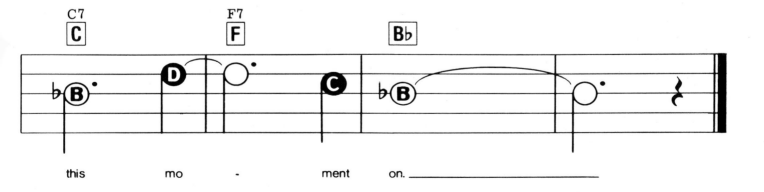

this   mo -   ment   on. _____

Hey, Good Lookin'

Registration 7
Rhythm: Rock or Swing

Words and Music by
Hank Williams

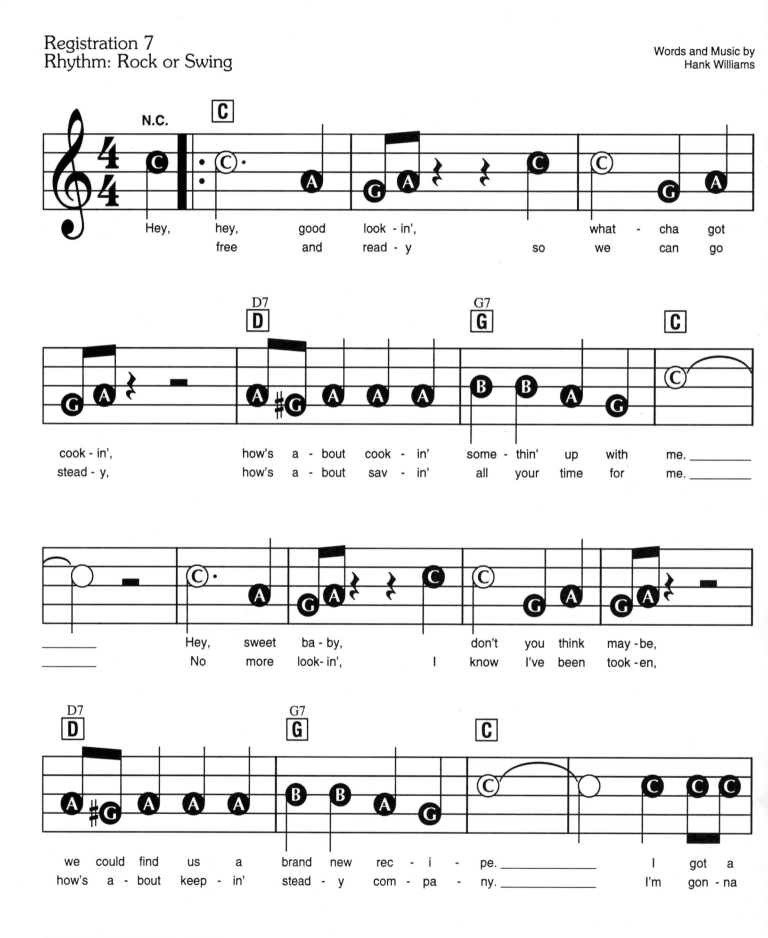

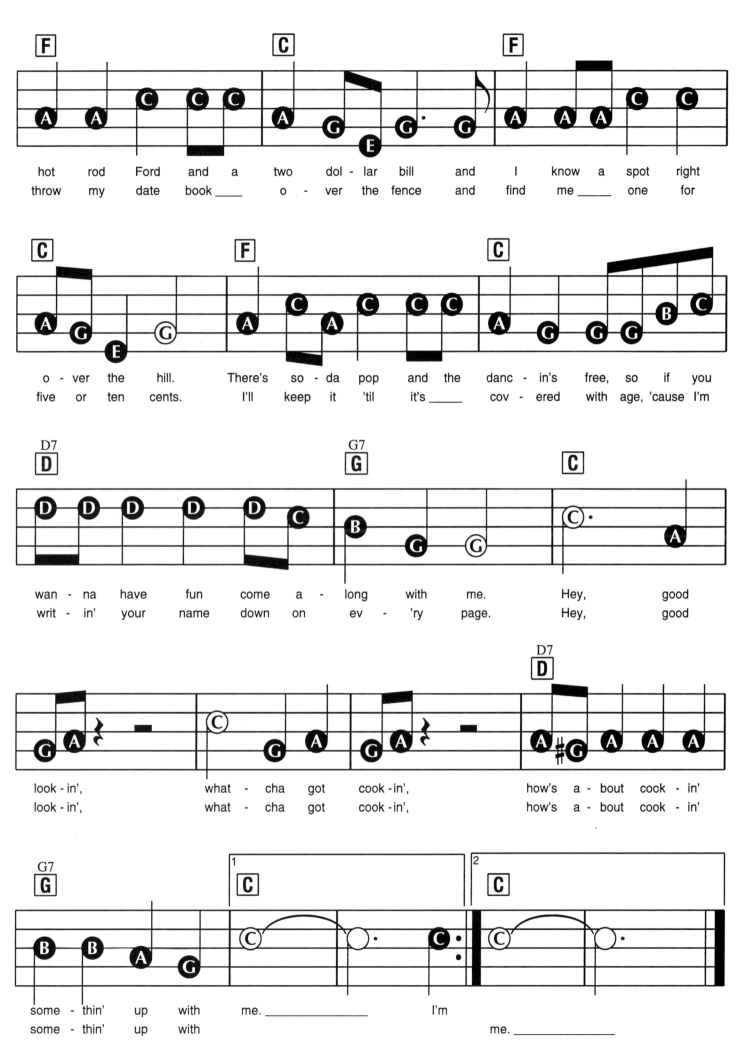

Hound Dog

Registration 7
Rhythm: Rock

Words and Music by Jerry Leiber
and Mike Stoller

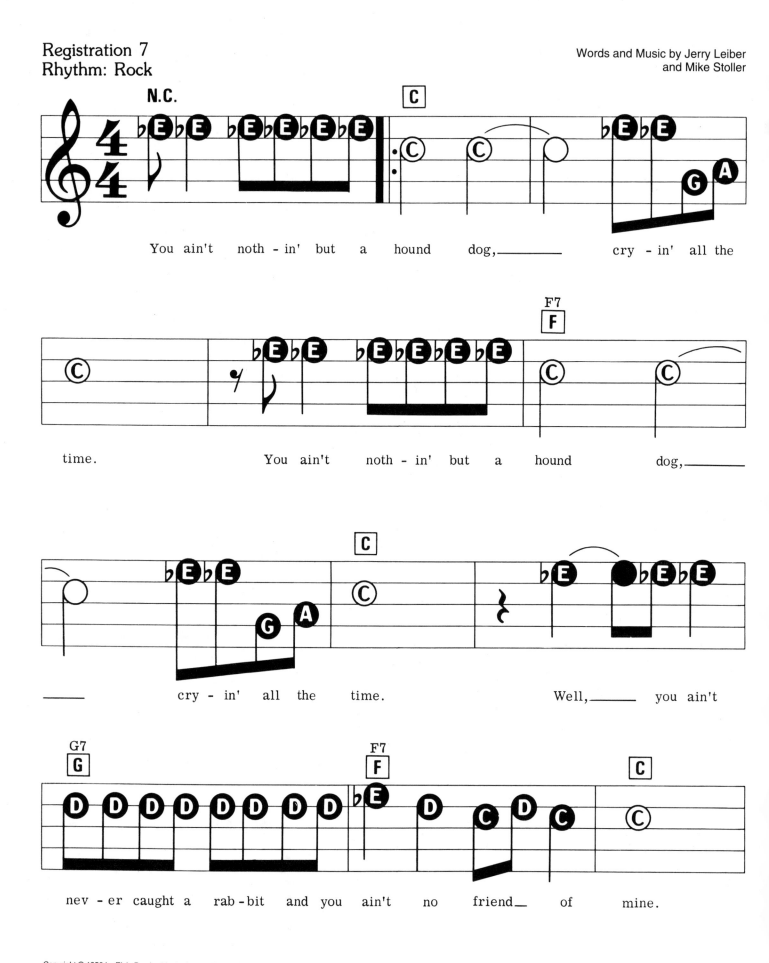

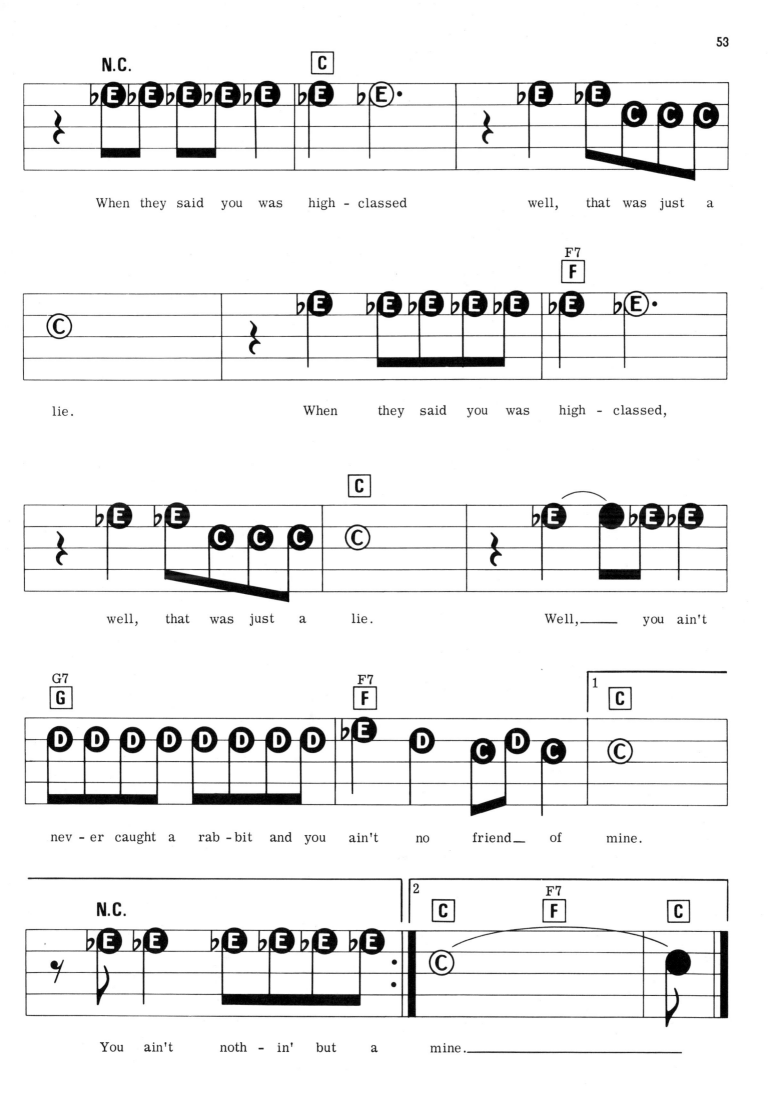

When they said you was high - classed well, that was just a

lie. When they said you was high - classed,

well, that was just a lie. Well,____ you ain't

nev - er caught a rab - bit and you ain't no friend___ of mine.

You ain't noth - in' but a mine.____

Hello, Young Lovers
(From "THE KING AND I")

Registration 1
Rhythm: Waltz

Lyrics by Oscar Hammerstein II
Music by Richard Rodgers

Hel - lo, young lov - ers, Who - ev - er you are, I
brave, young lov - ers, And fol - low your star, Be

hope your trou - bles are few
brave and faith - ful are and true

All my good wish - es go with you to - night
Cling ver - y close to each oth - er to - night

I've been in love like you
I've been in love like

Be

55

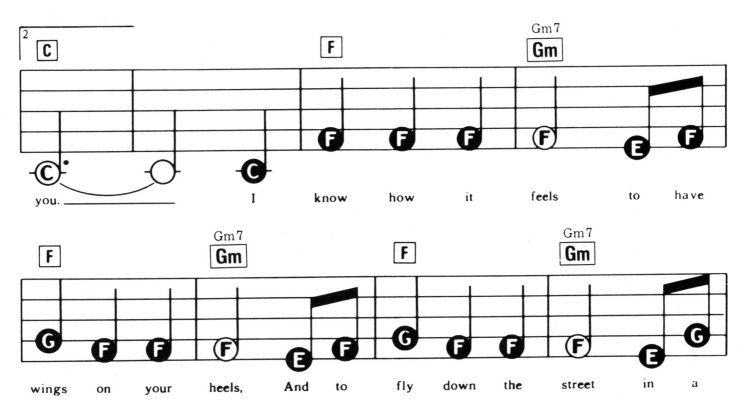

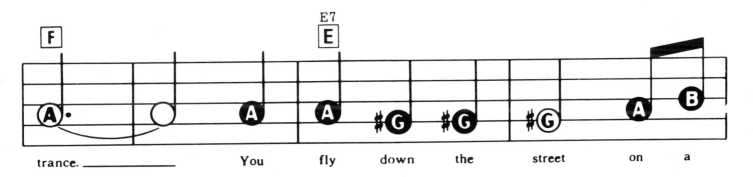

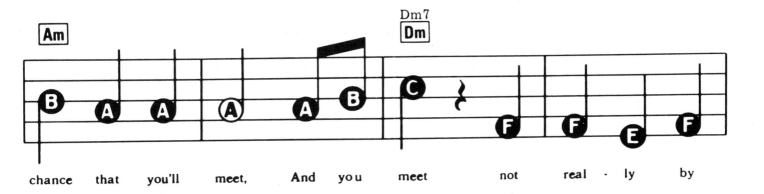

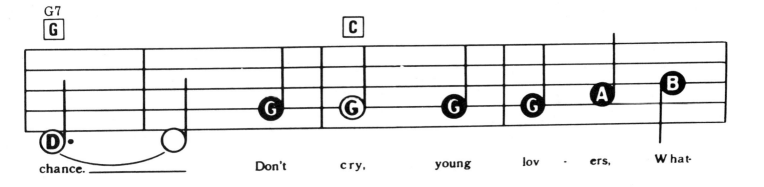

56

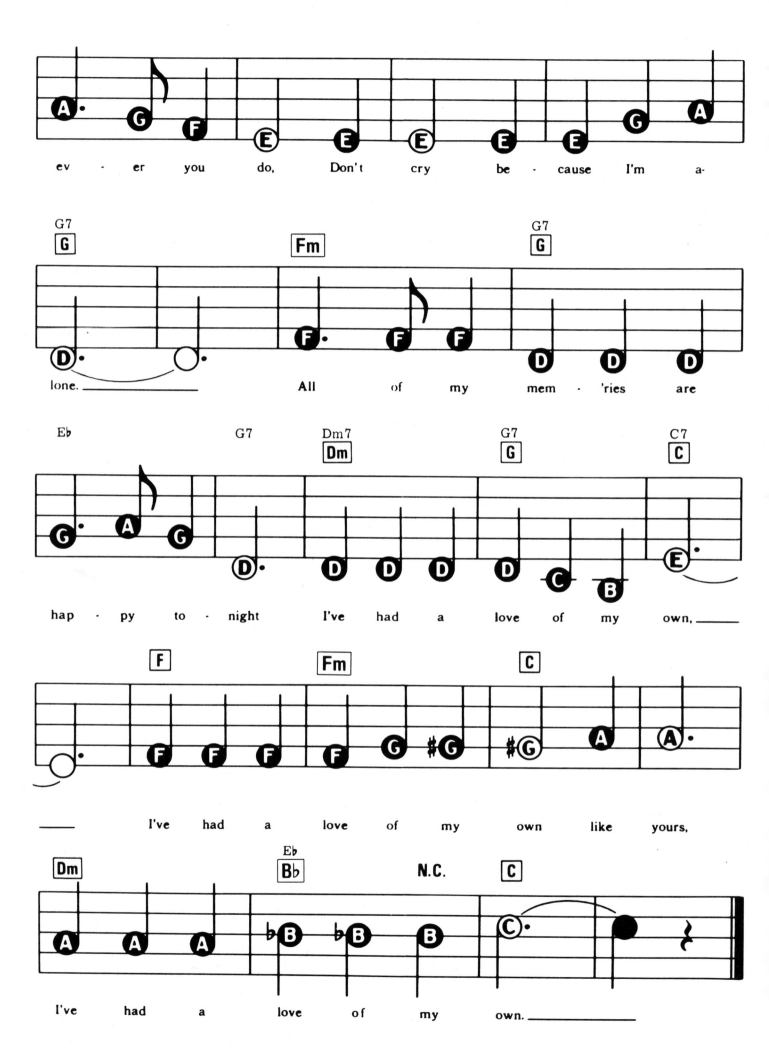

I Am In Love

Registration 8
Rhythm: Bossa Nova or Fox Trot

Words and Music by
Cole Porter

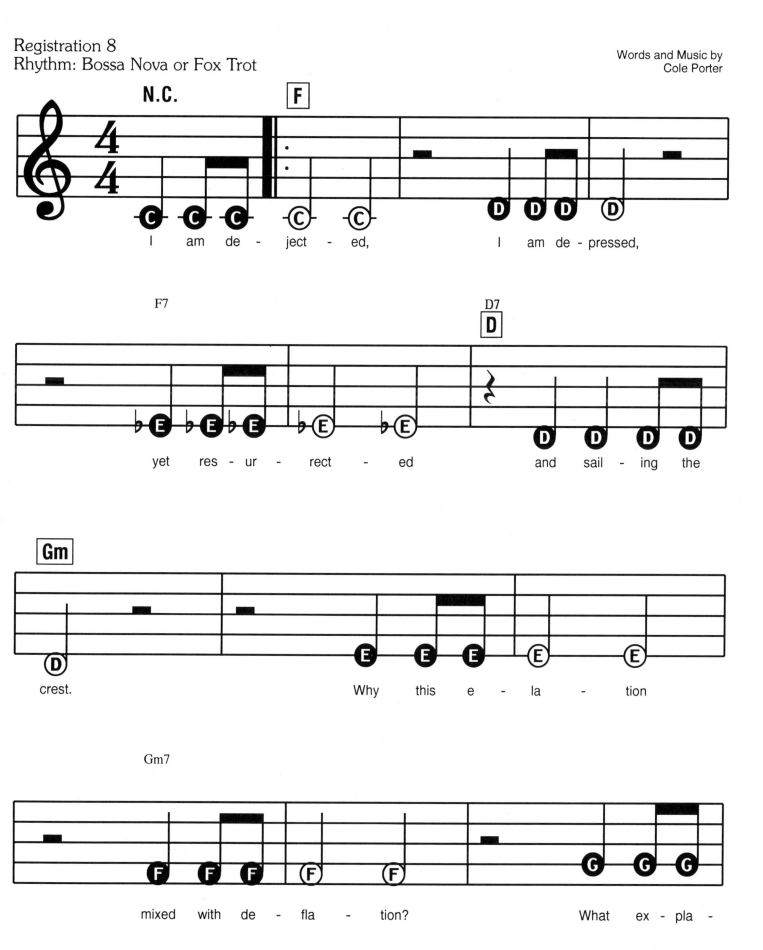

58

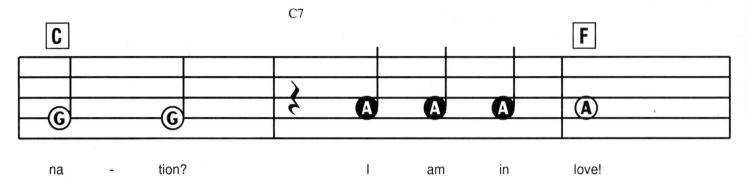

na - tion?   I am in love!

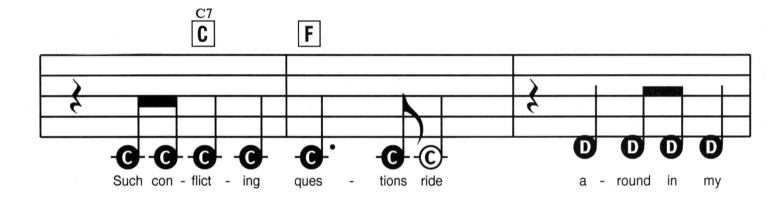

Such con - flict - ing   ques - tions ride   a - round in my

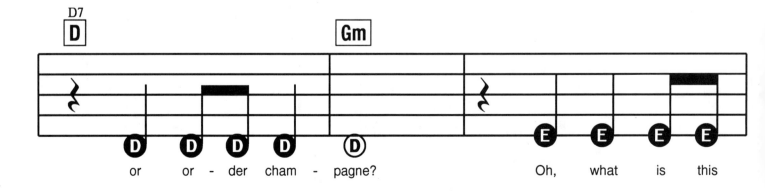

brain.   Should I or - der   cy - a - nide

or or - der cham - pagne?   Oh, what is this

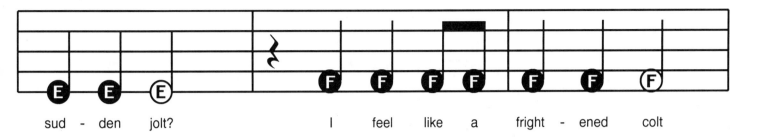

Gm7

sud - den jolt?   I feel like a fright - ened colt

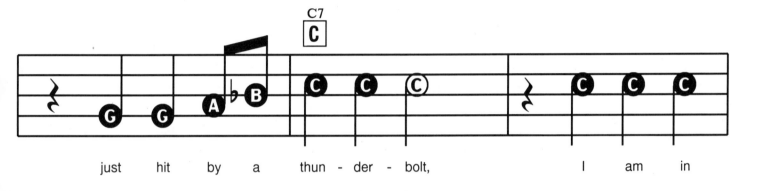

C7

just hit by a thun - der - bolt,   I am in

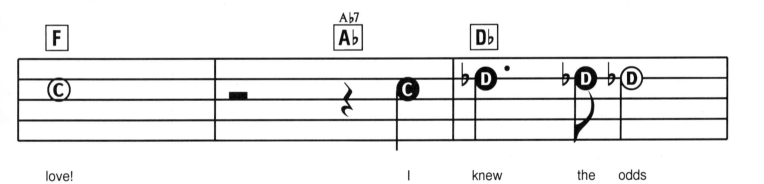

F   Ab7   Db

love!   I knew the odds

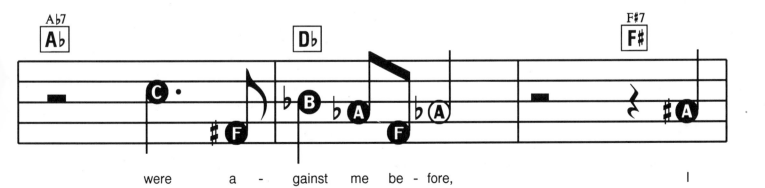

Ab7   Db   F#7

were a - gainst me be - fore,   I

60

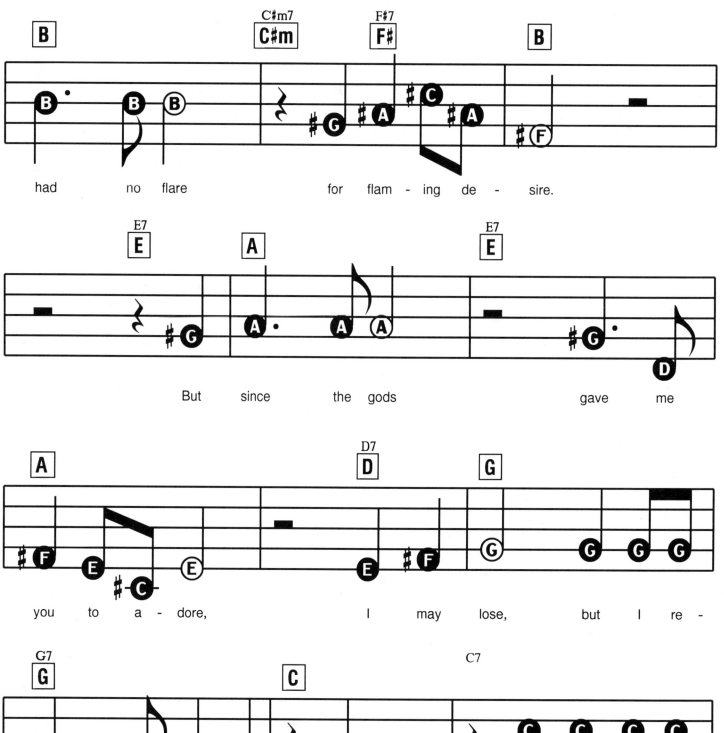

had no flare for flam - ing de - sire.

But since the gods gave me

you to a - dore, I may lose, but I re -

fuse to fight the fire! So, come an en -

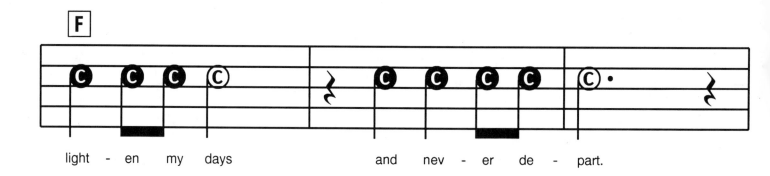

light - en my days and nev - er de - part.

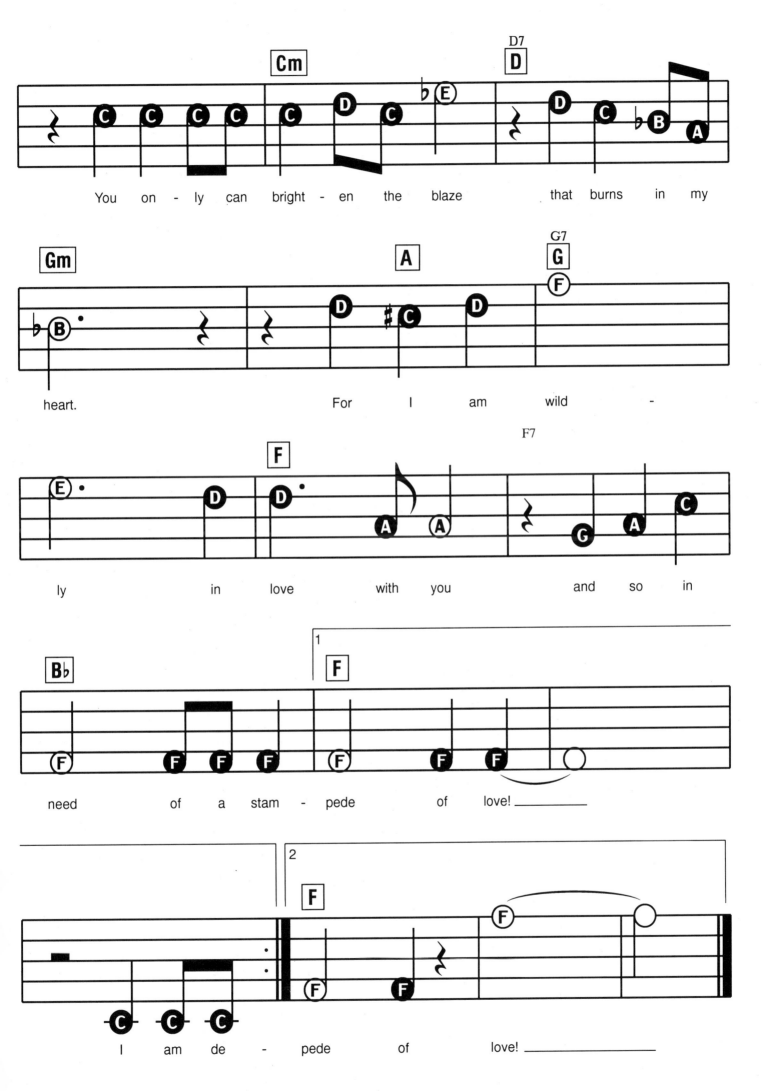

I Could Have Danced All Night

(From "MY FAIR LADY")

Registration 4
Rhythm: Beguine

Words by Alan Jay Lerner
Music by Frederick Loewe

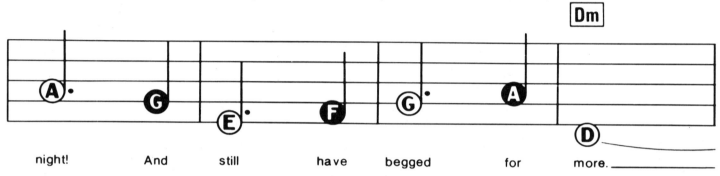

I could have danced all night! I could have danced all

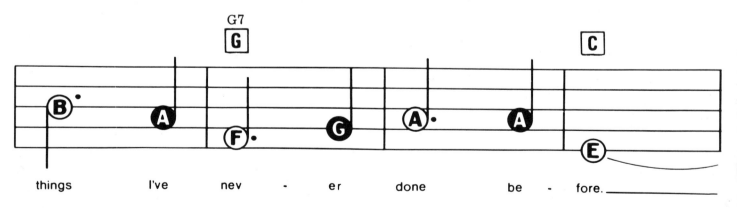

night! And still have begged for more.____

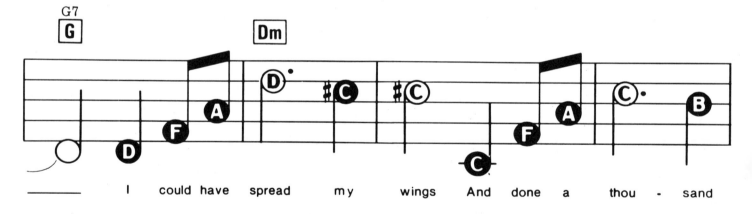

____ I could have spread my wings And done a thou - sand

things I've nev - er done be - fore.____

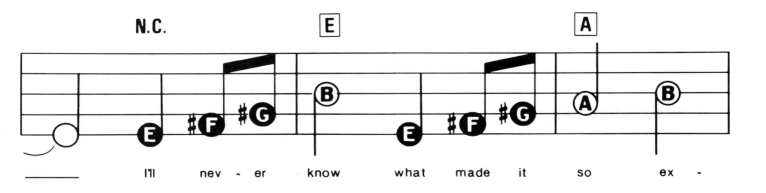

I'll nev - er know what made it so ex -

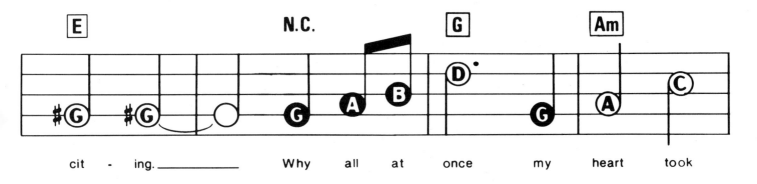

cit - ing._____ Why all at once my heart took

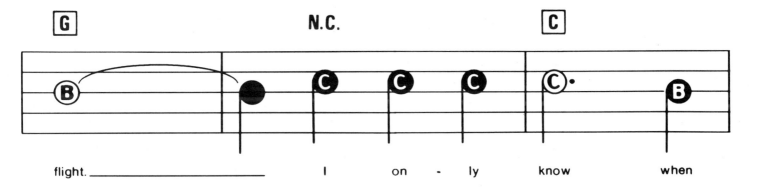

flight._____ I on - ly know when

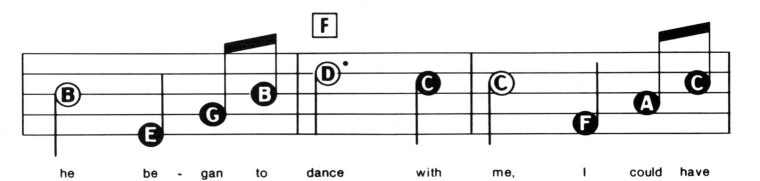

he be - gan to dance with me, I could have

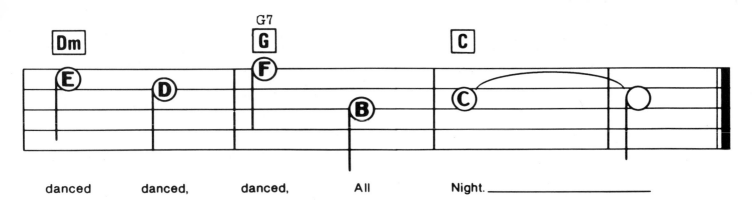

danced danced, danced, All Night._____

I Left My Heart In San Francisco

Registration 9
Rhythm: Fox Trot

Words by Douglas Cross
Music by George Cory

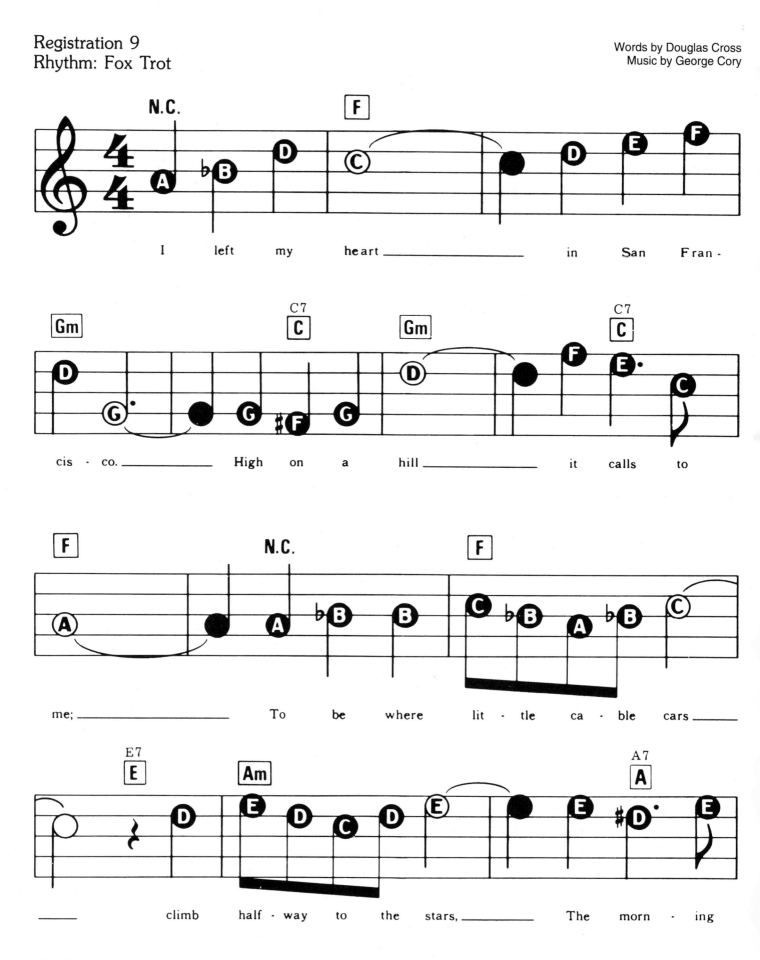

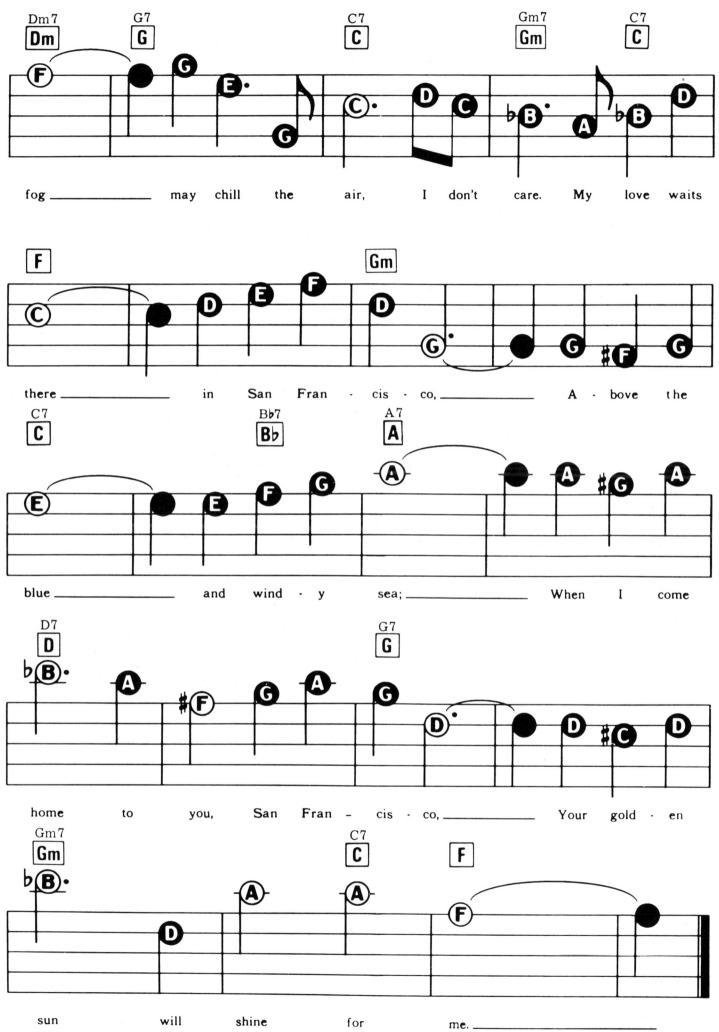

I Wanna Be Loved

Registration 2
Rhythm: Fox Trot or Swing

Words by Billy Rose and Edward Heyman
Music by Johnny Green

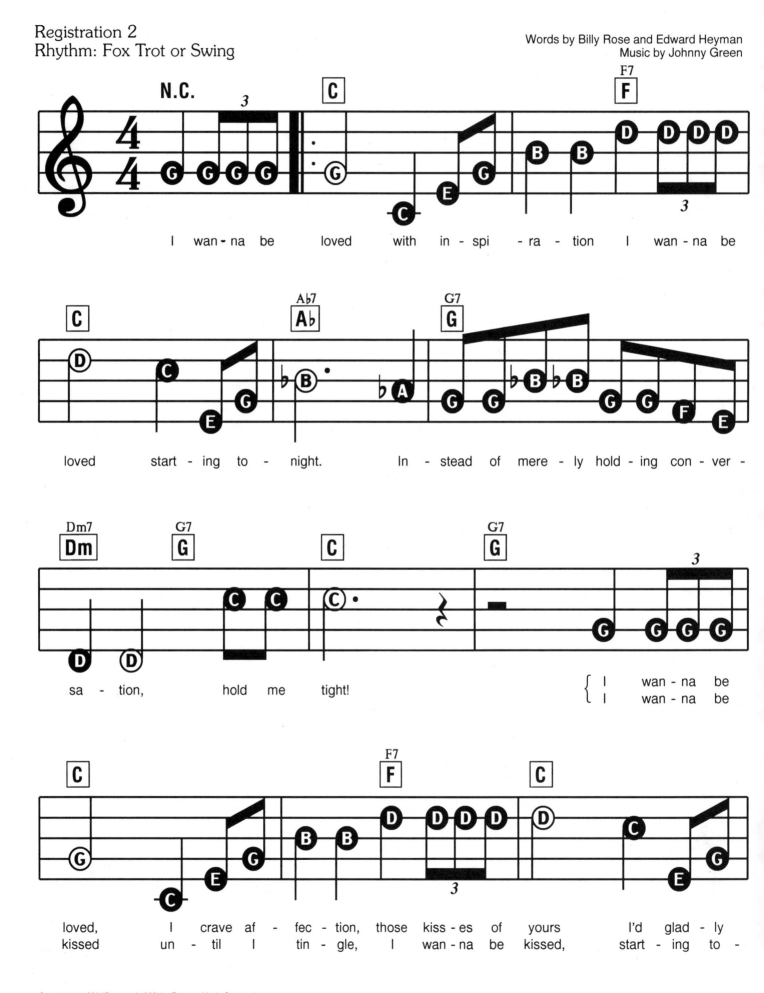

ren - der." _____ I wan - na be thrilled by on - ly
lov - ing. _____ I wan - na be thrilled to des - per -

you dear, I wan - na be thrilled by your ca -
a - tion, I wan - na be thrilled start - ing to -

ress. I wan - na find each dream of mine come
night. With ev - 'ry kind of won - der - ful sen -

true dear, I wan - na be loved!
sa - tion, I wan - na be

I wan - na be loved! _____

I've Grown Accustomed To Her Face
(From "MY FAIR LADY")

Registration 7
Rhythm: 8 Beat or Pops

Words by Alan Jay Lerner
Music by Frederick Loewe

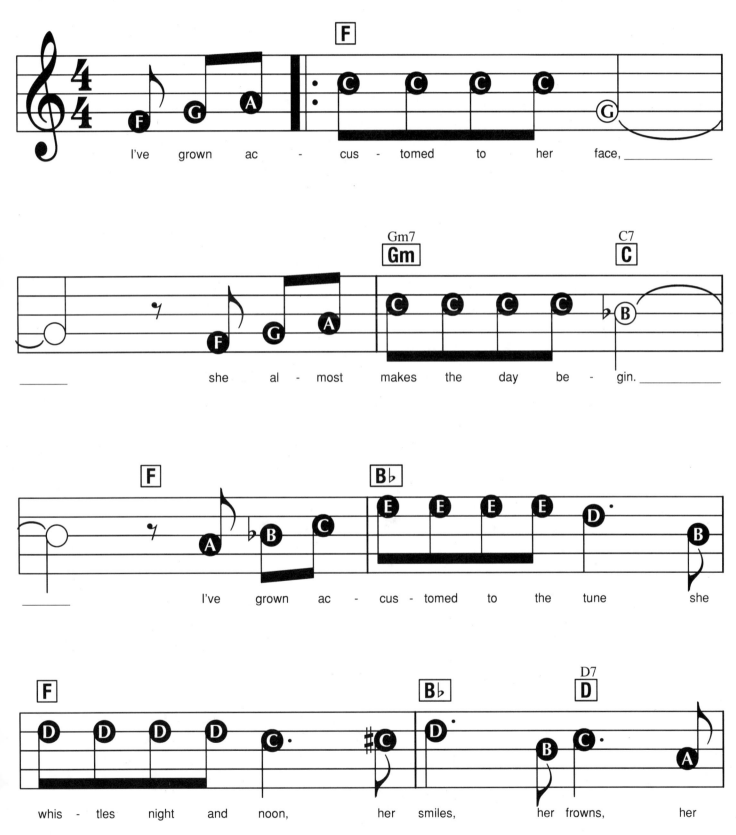

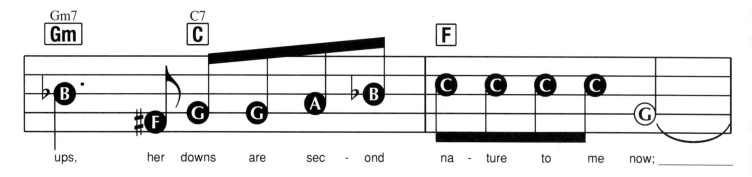

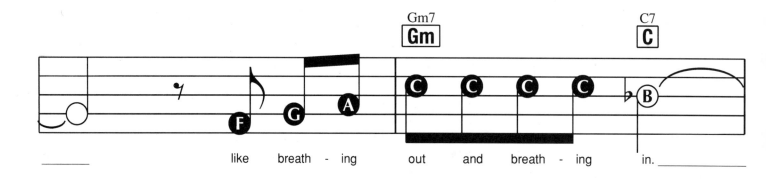

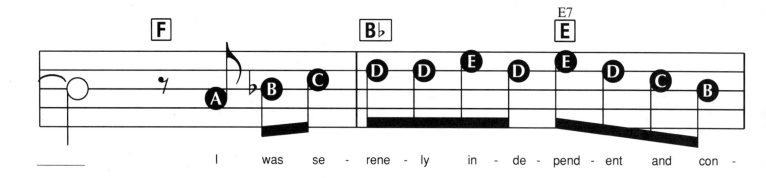

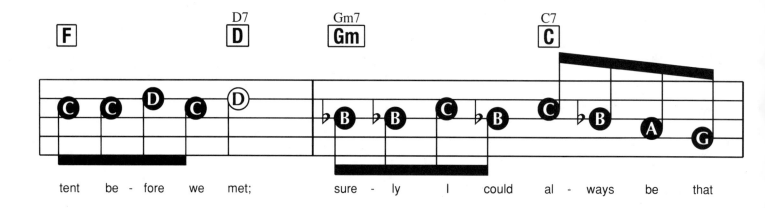

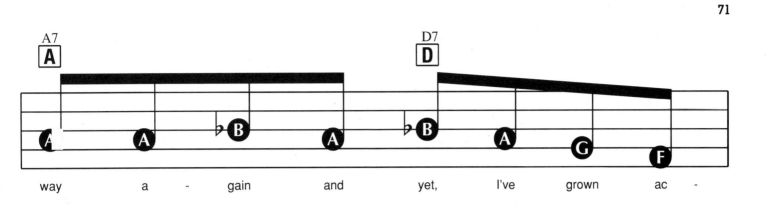

way a - gain and yet, I've grown ac -

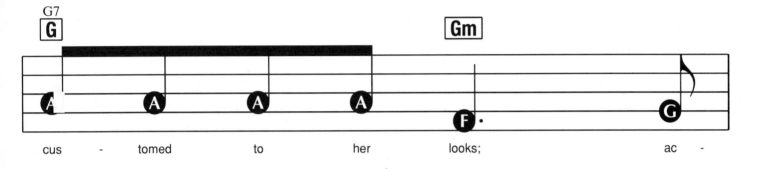

cus - tomed to her looks; ac -

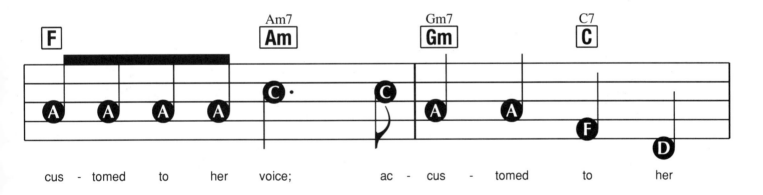

cus - tomed to her voice; ac - cus - tomed to her

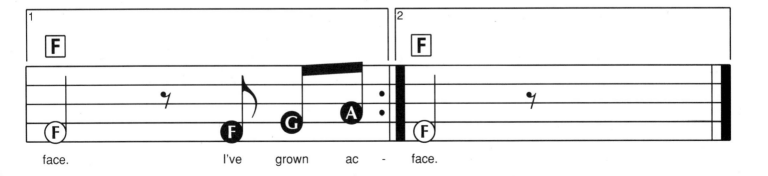

face. I've grown ac - face.

I Whistle A Happy Tune
(From "THE KING AND I")

Registration 1
Rhythm: Fox Trot or Swing

Lyrics by Oscar Hammerstein II
Music by Richard Rodgers

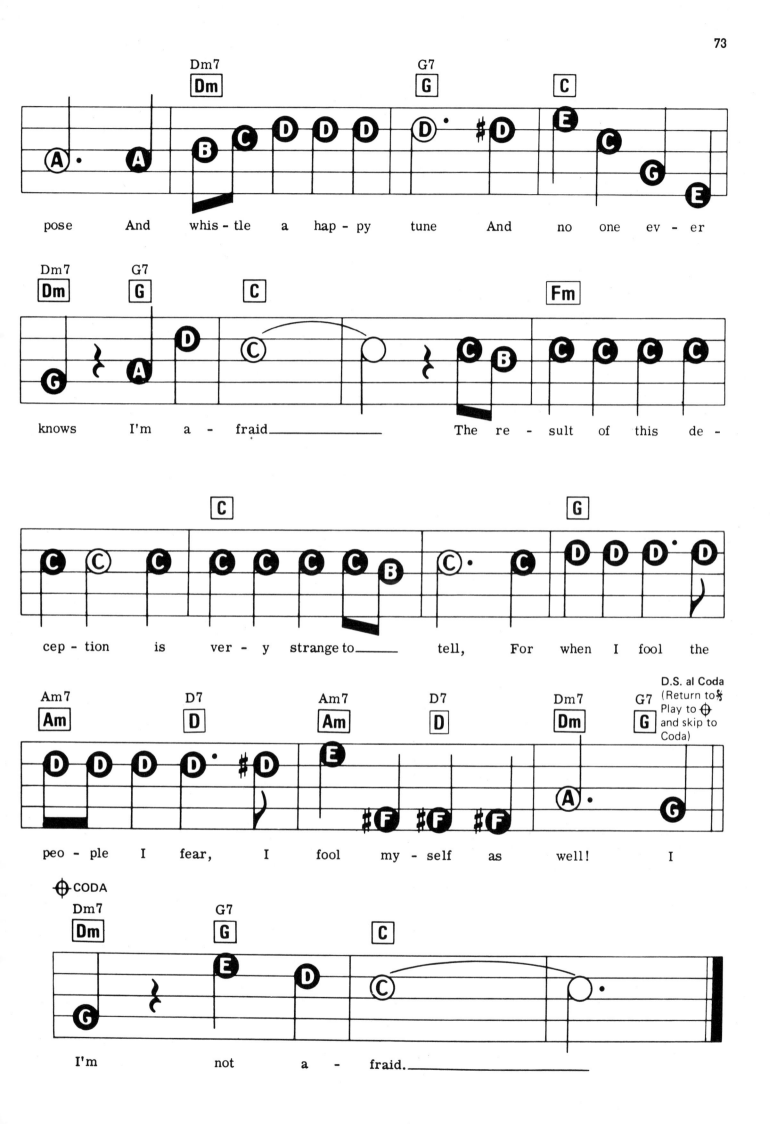

It's All Right With Me
(From "CAN-CAN")

Registration 3
Rhythm: Swing or Fox Trot

Words and Music by
Cole Porter

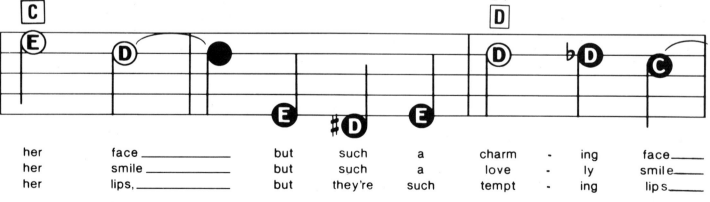

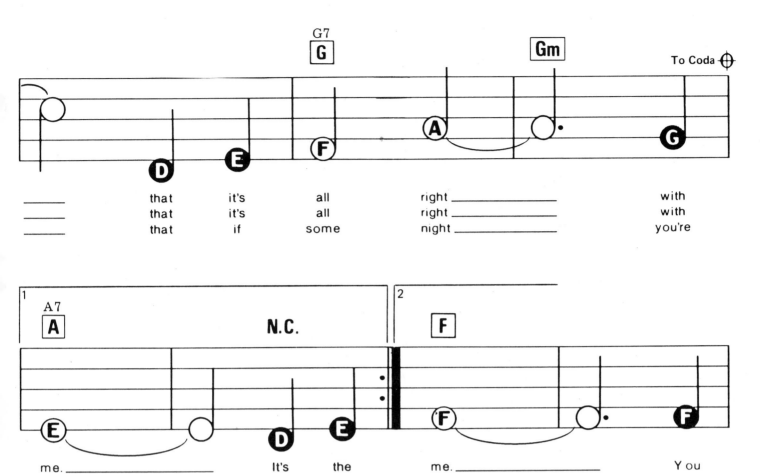

that   it's   all   right _____ with
that   it's   all   right _____ with
that   if   some   night _____ you're

me. _____   It's   the   me. _____ You

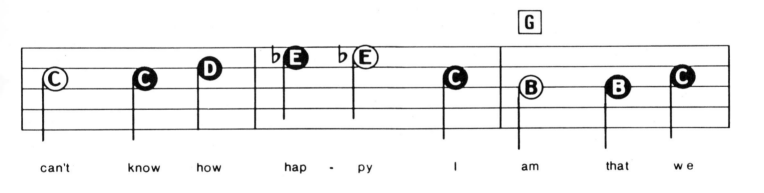

can't   know   how   hap - py   I   am   that   we

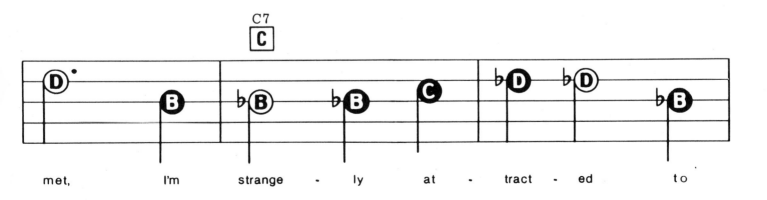

met,   I'm   strange - ly   at - tract - ed   to

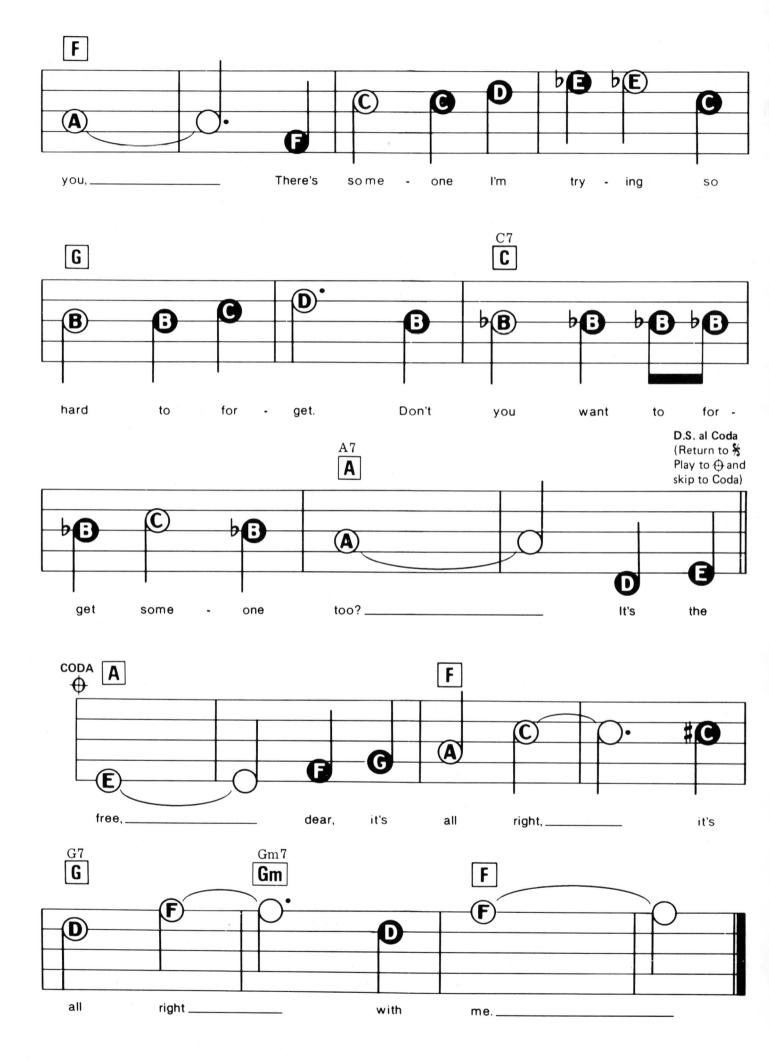

Kiss Of Fire

Registration 5
Rhythm: Tango or Latin

Words and Music by Lester Allen
and Robert Hill
(Adapted from A.G. Villoldo)

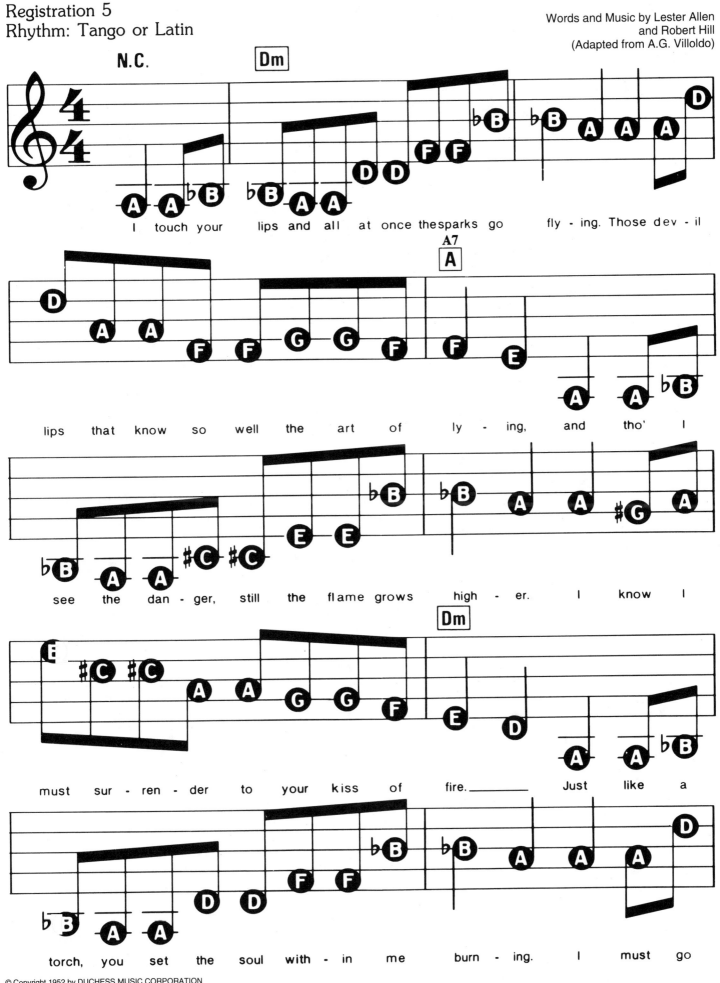

MCA music publishing

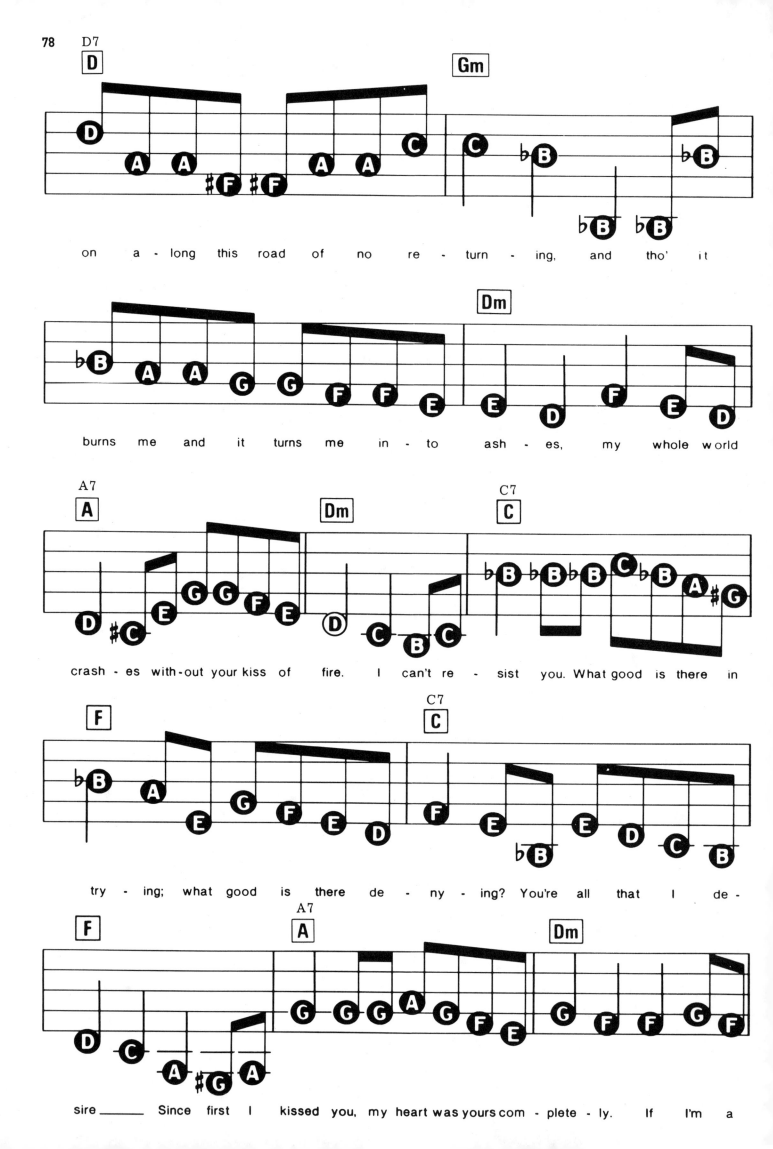

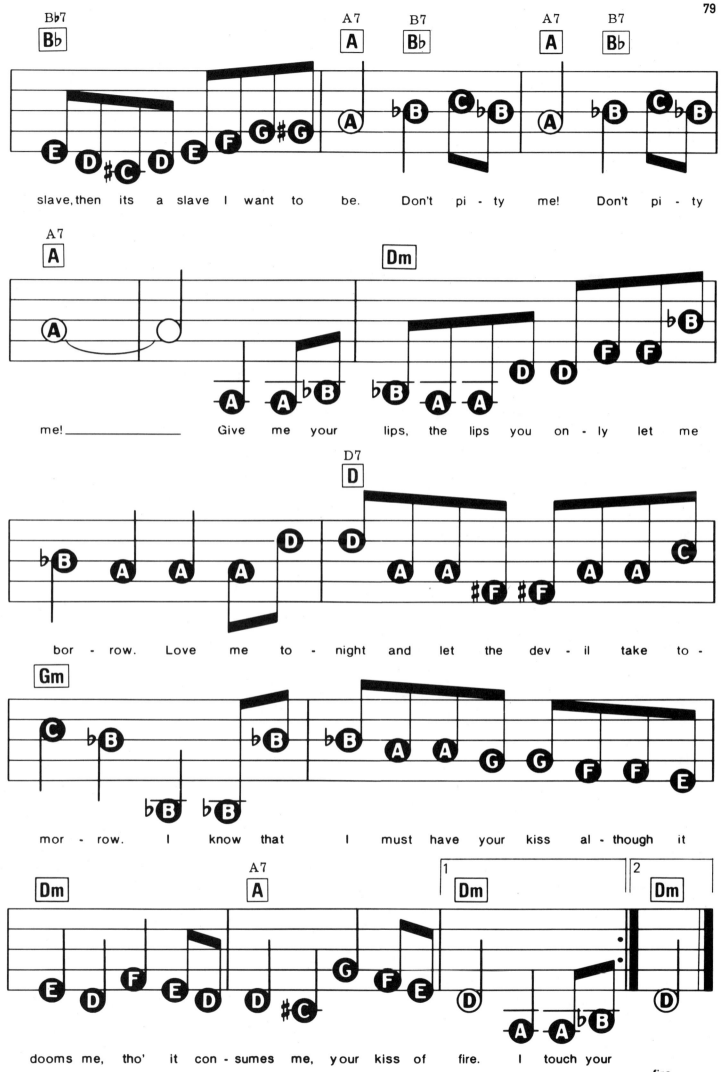

Lazy Afternoon

Registration 9
Rhythm: Pops or 8 Beat

Words by John Latouche
Music by Jerome Moross

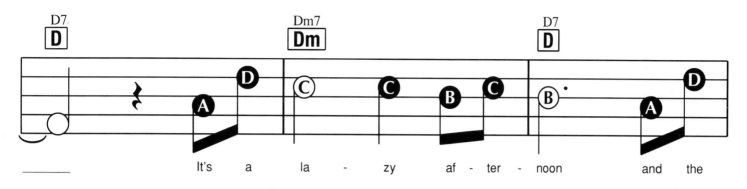

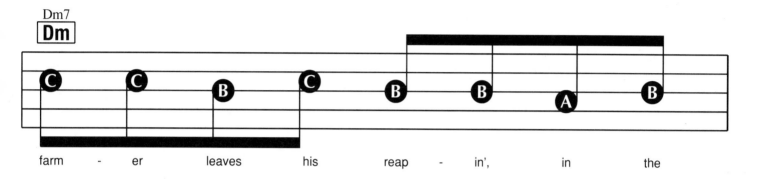

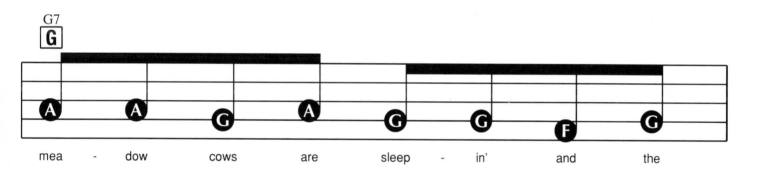

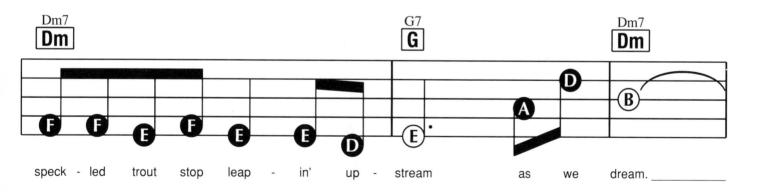

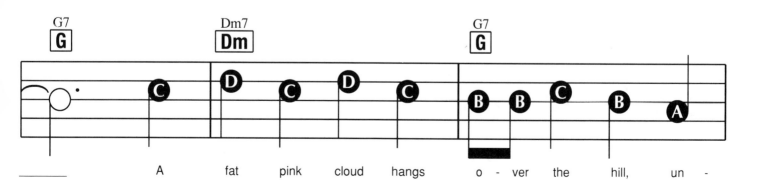

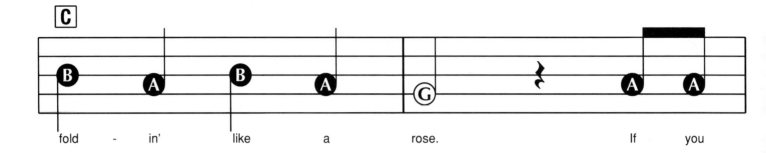

fold - in' like a rose. If you

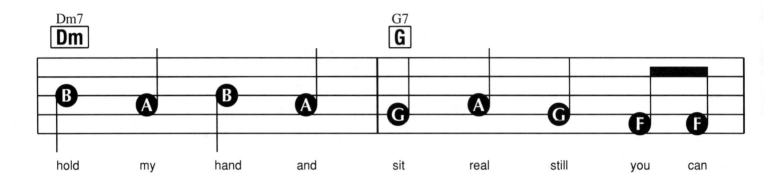

hold my hand and sit real still you can

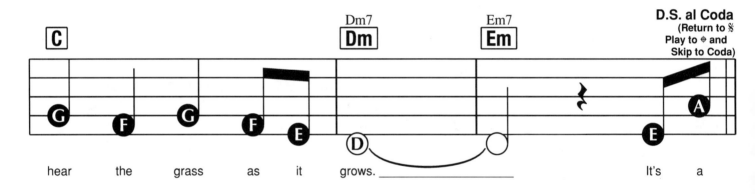

hear the grass as it grows. It's a

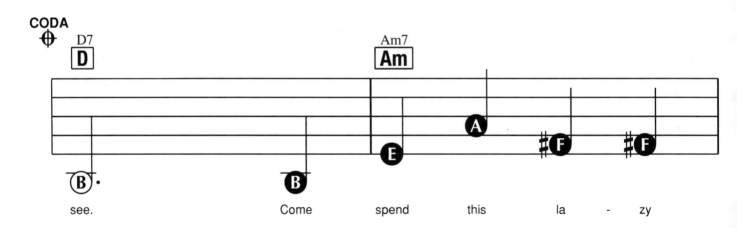

see. Come spend this la - zy

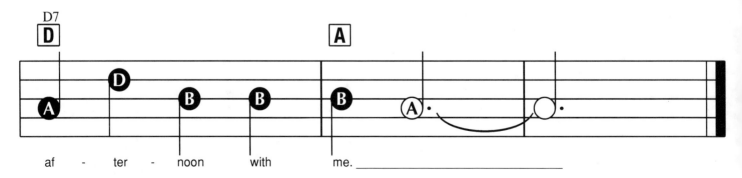

af - ter - noon with me.

Love and Marriage

Registration 1
Rhythm: Swing or Big Band

Words by Sammy Cahn
Music by James Van Heusen

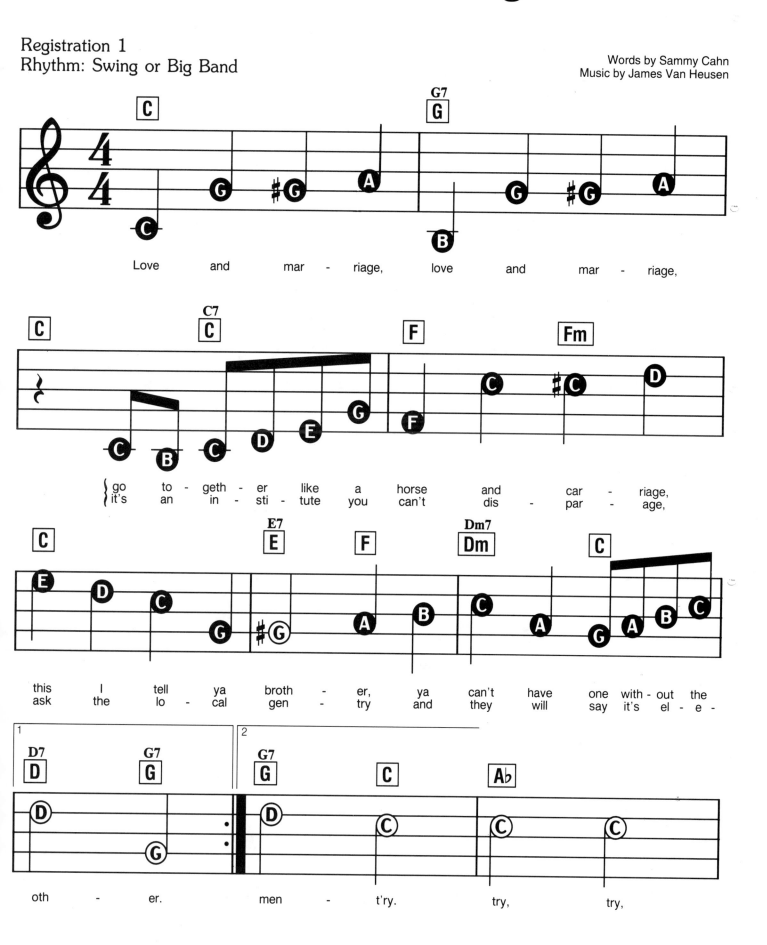

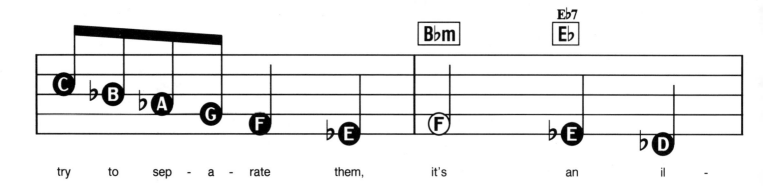

try to sep - a - rate them, it's an il -

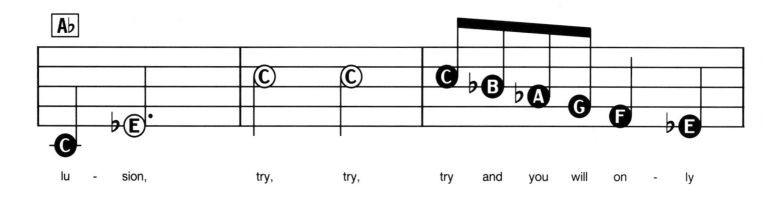

lu - sion, try, try, try and you will on - ly

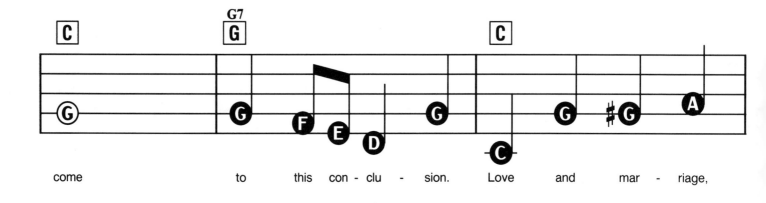

come to this con - clu - sion. Love and mar - riage,

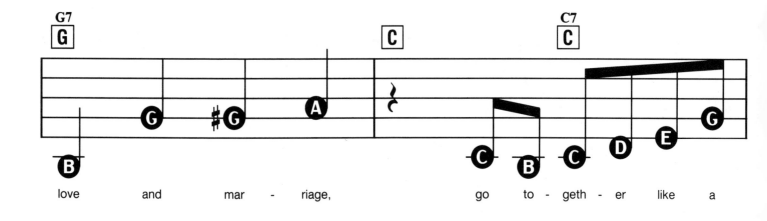

love and mar - riage, go to - geth - er like a

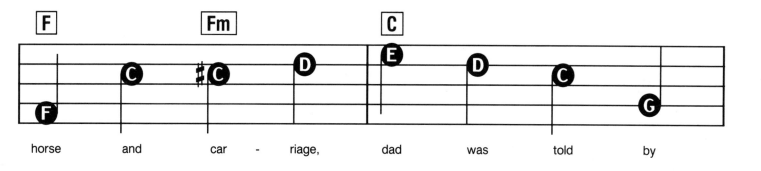

horse and car - riage, dad was told by

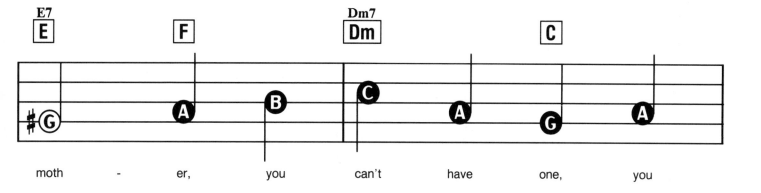

moth - er, you can't have one, you

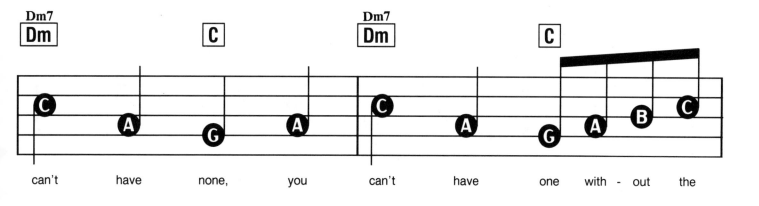

can't have none, you can't have one with - out the

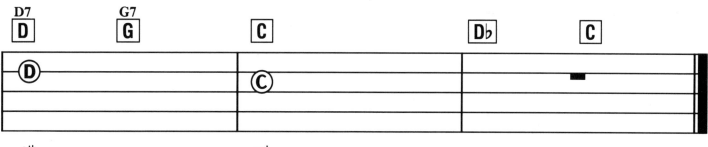

oth - er!

Long Before I Knew You
(From "BELLS ARE RINGING")

Words by Betty Comden and Adolph Green
Music by Jule Styne

Registration 2
Rhythm: Ballad

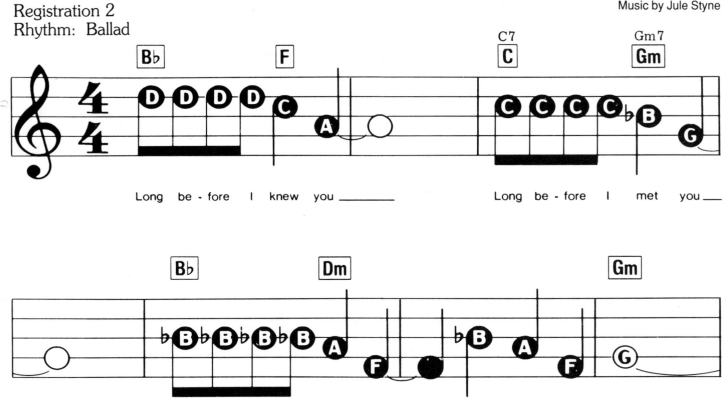

Long be-fore I knew you _____ Long be-fore I met you _____

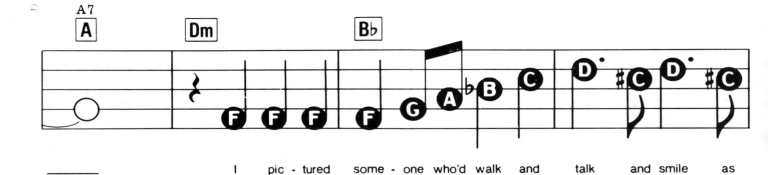

_____ I was sure I'd find you _____ some-day, some-how. _____

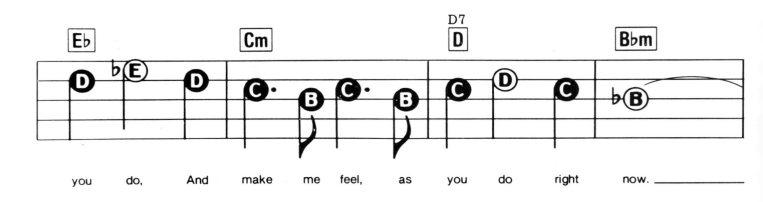

I pic-tured some-one who'd walk and talk and smile as

you do, And make me feel, as you do right now. _____

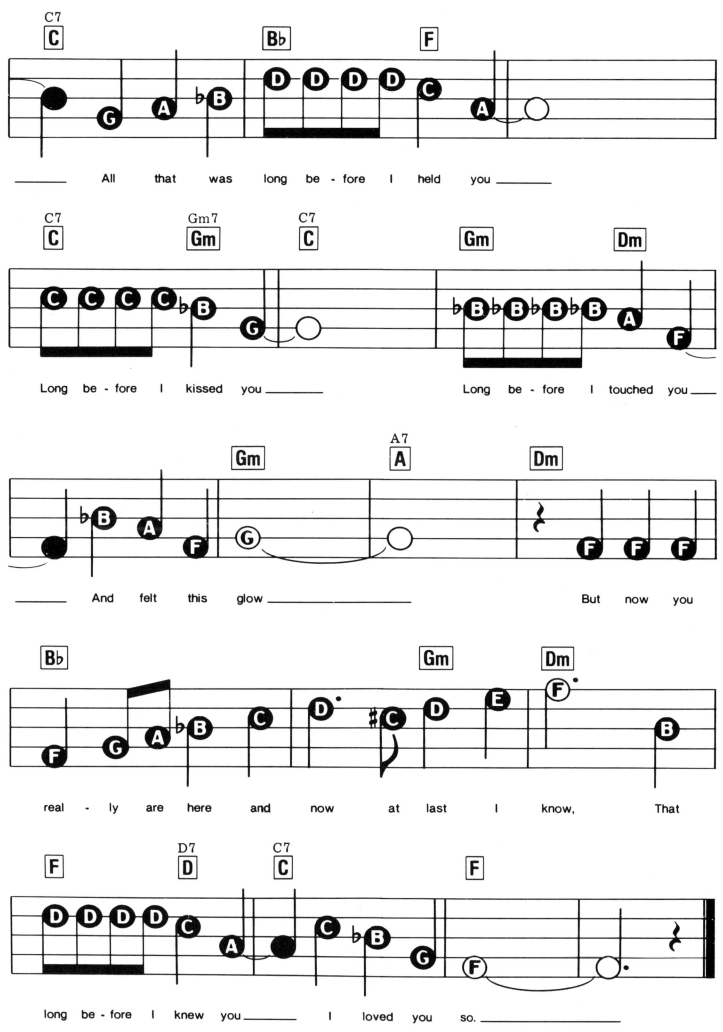

Love, Look Away
(From "FLOWER DRUM SONG")

Registration 7
Rhythm: Pops or 8-Beat

Lyrics by Oscar Hammerstein II
Music by Richard Rodgers

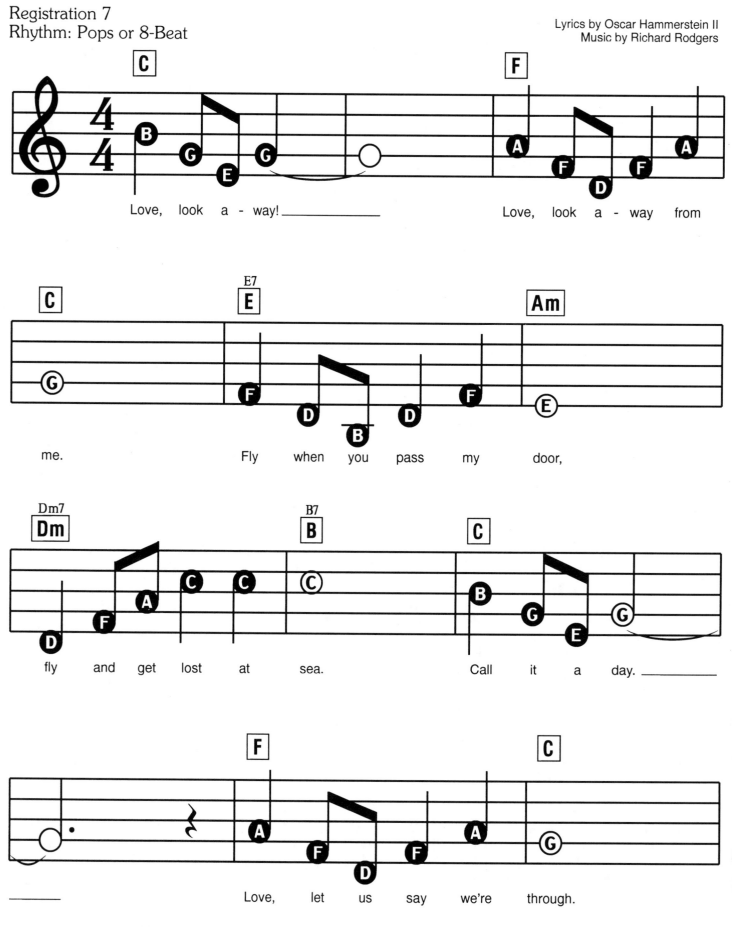

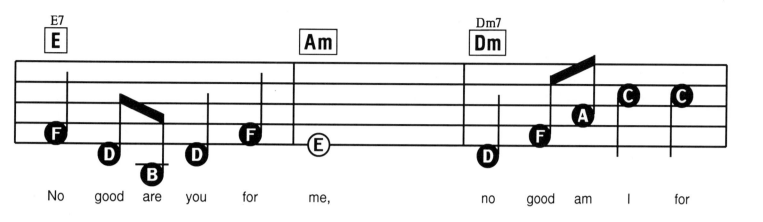

No good are you for me, no good am I for

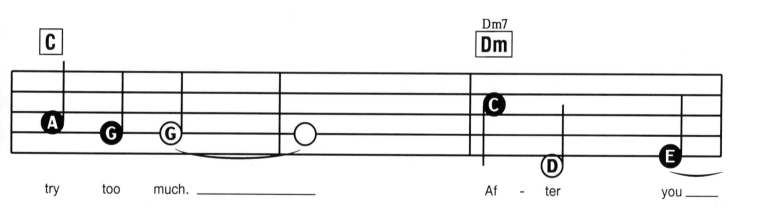

you. Want - ing you _____ so, I

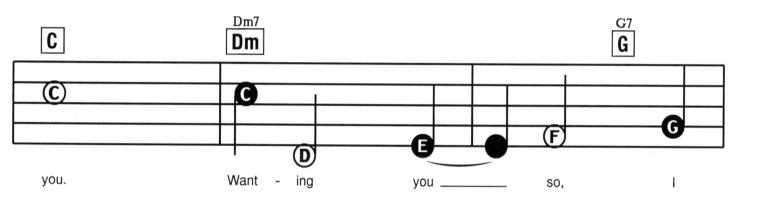

try too much. _____ Af - ter you ____

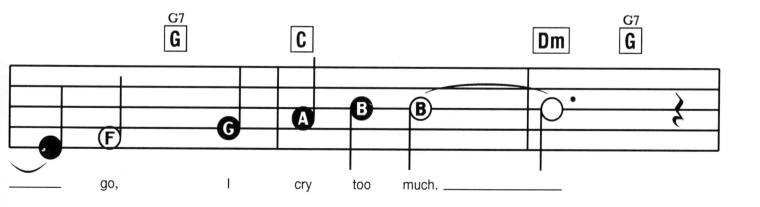

_____ go, I cry too much. _____

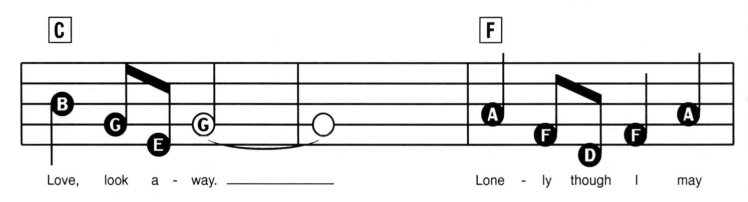

Love, look a - way. _____ Lone - ly though I may

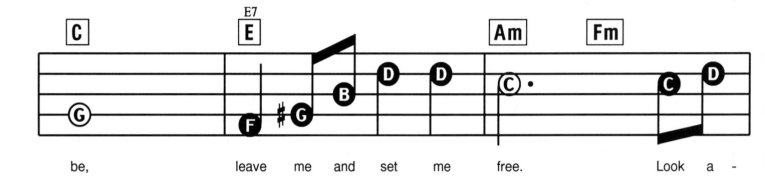

be, leave me and set me free. Look a -

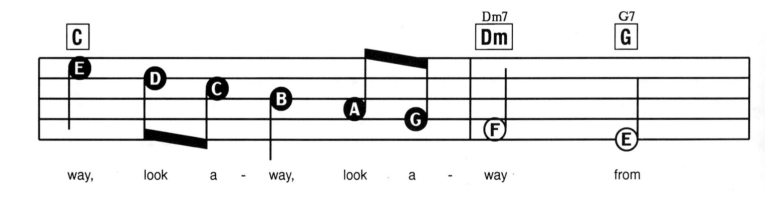

way, look a - way, look a - way from

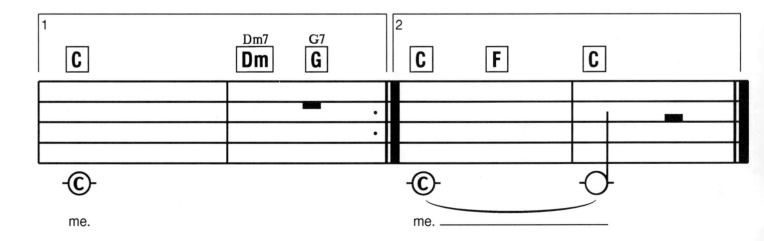

me. me. _____

(You've Got) Personality

Registration 5
Rhythm: Shuffle or Swing

Words and Music by Harold Logan
and Lloyd Price

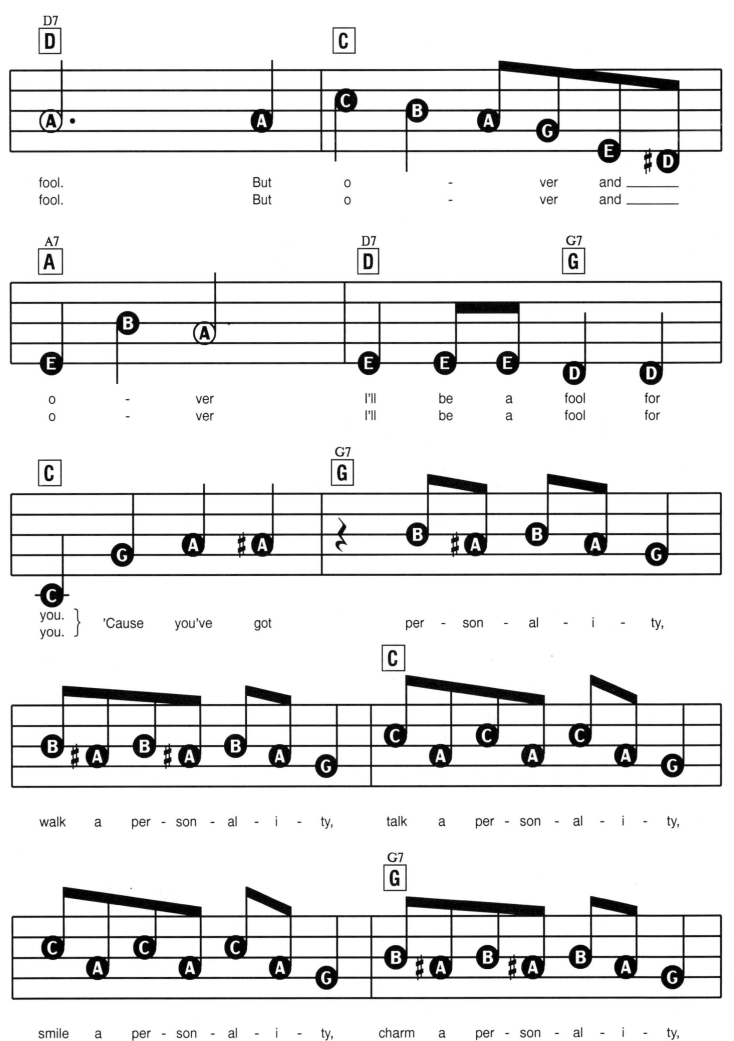

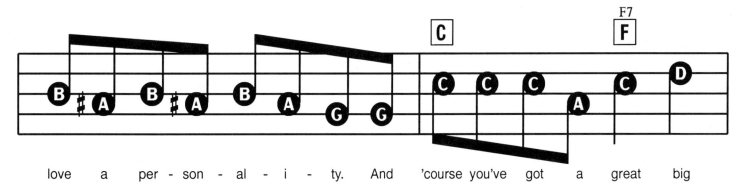

love a per-son-al-i-ty. And 'course you've got a great big

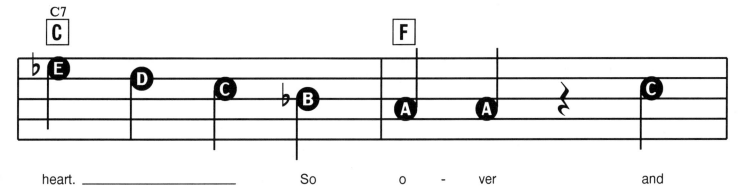

heart. _____ So o - ver and

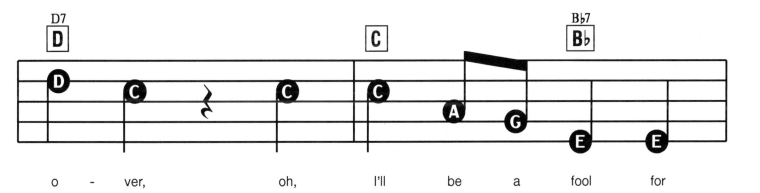

o - ver, oh, I'll be a fool for

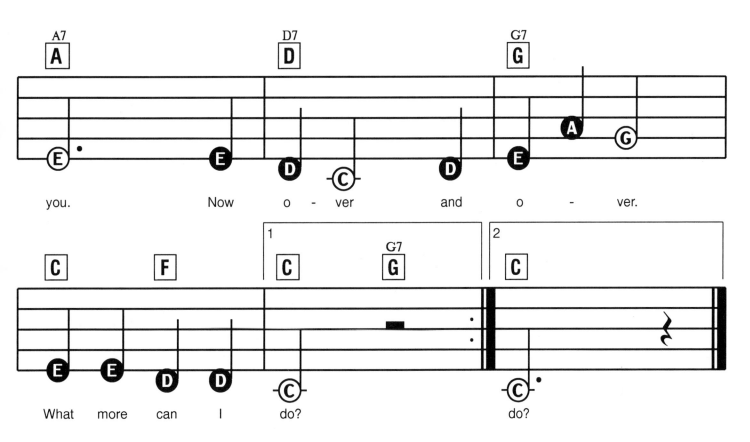

you. Now o - ver and o - ver.

What more can I do? do?

Mack The Knife

English Words by Marc Blitzstein
Original German Words by Bert Brecht
Music by Kurt Weill

Registration 8
Rhythm: Swing

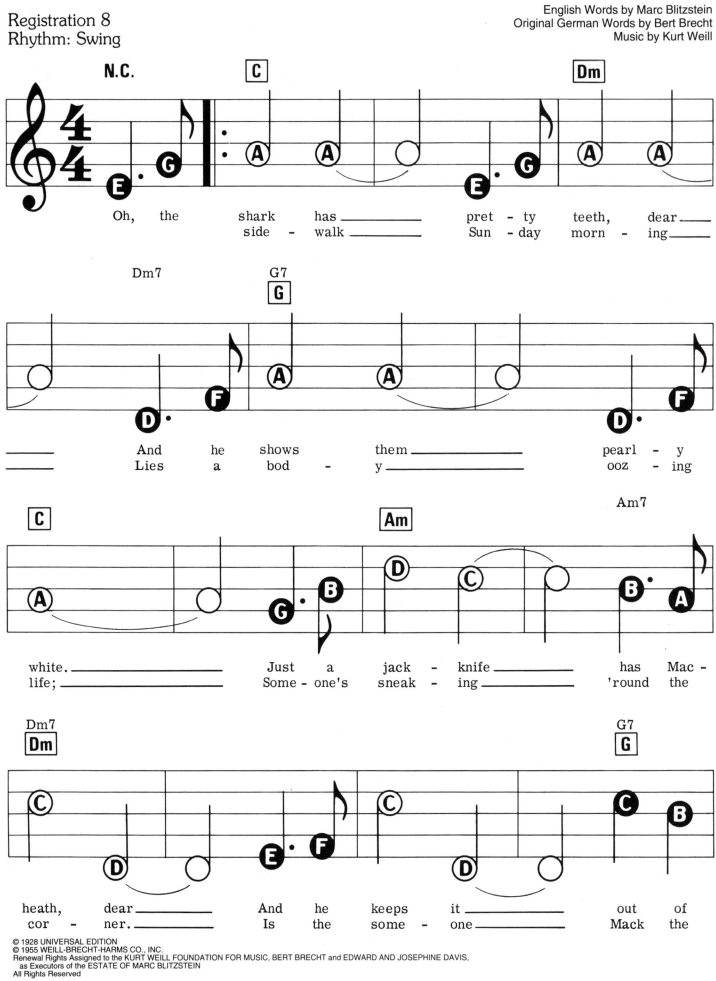

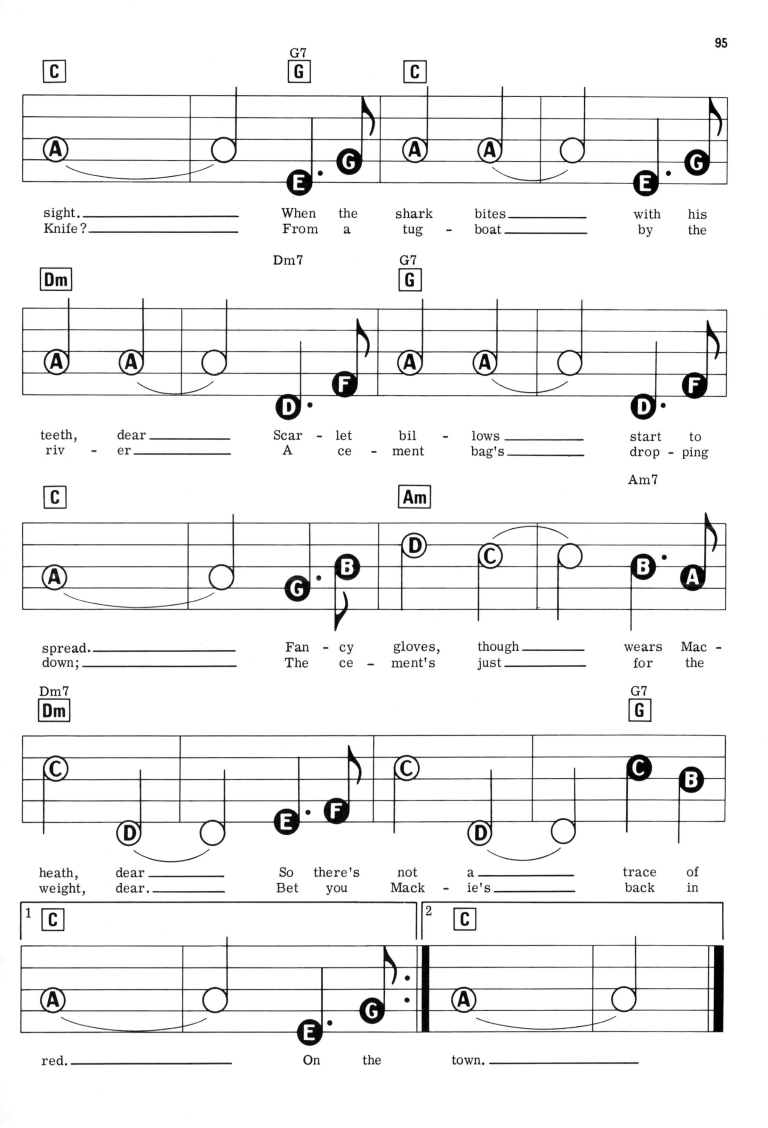

Magic Moments

Registration 9
Rhythm: Swing or Shuffle

Lyric by Hal David
Music by Burt Bacharach

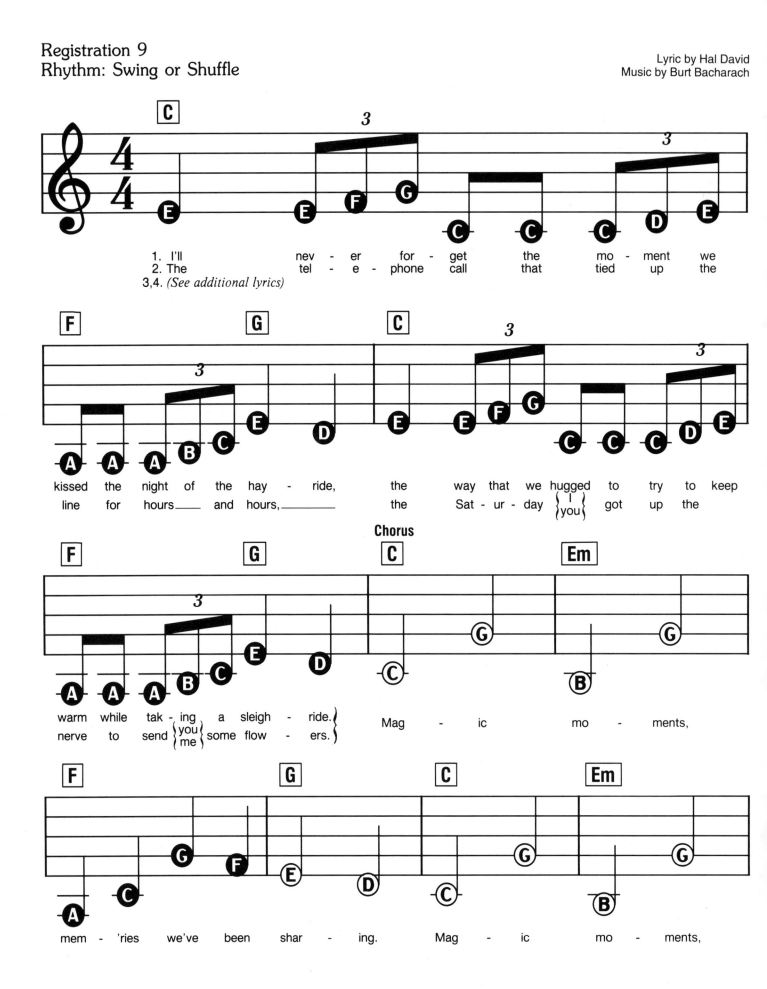

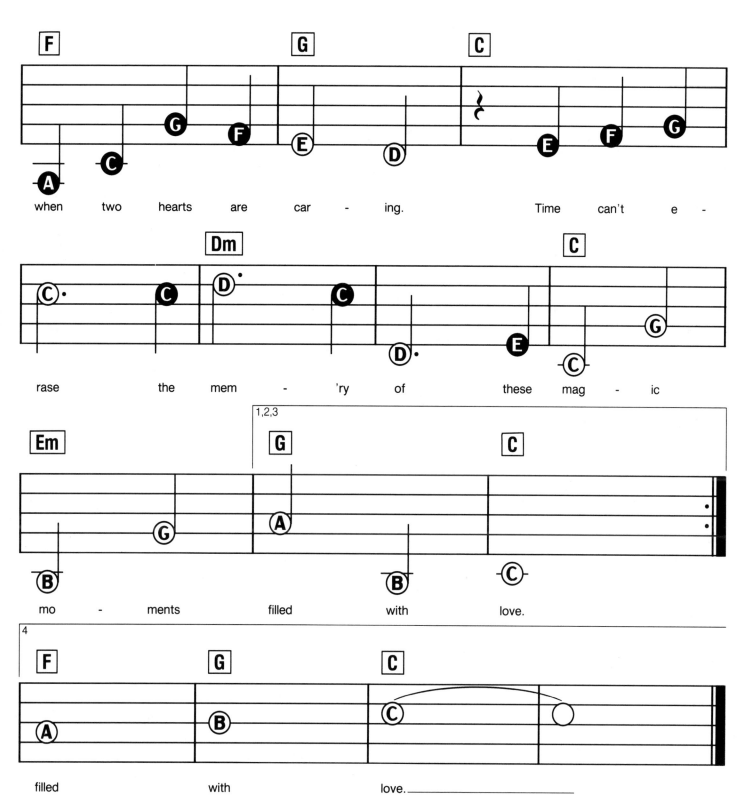

when   two   hearts   are   car - ing.   Time   can't   e -

rase   the   mem -   'ry   of   these   mag - ic

mo -   ments   filled   with   love.

filled   with   love.

Additional Lyrics

3. The way that we cheered whenever our team was scoring a touchdown,
   The time that the floor fell out of { my / your } car when { I / you } put the clutch down;
   (To Chorus)

4. The penny arcade, the games that we played, the fun and the prizes,
   The Halloween hop when ev'ryone came in funny disguises;
   (To Chorus)

Mona Lisa
(From The Paramount Picture "CAPTAIN CAREY, U.S.A.")

Registration 9
Rhythm: Swing or 8 Beat

Words and Music by Jay Livingston
and Ray Evans

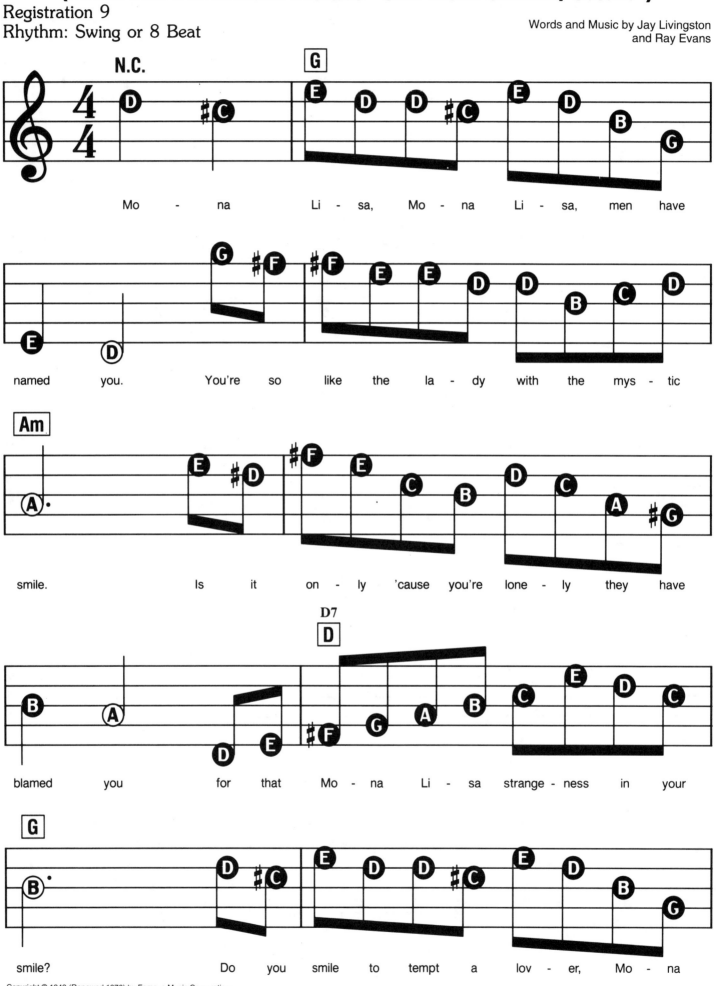

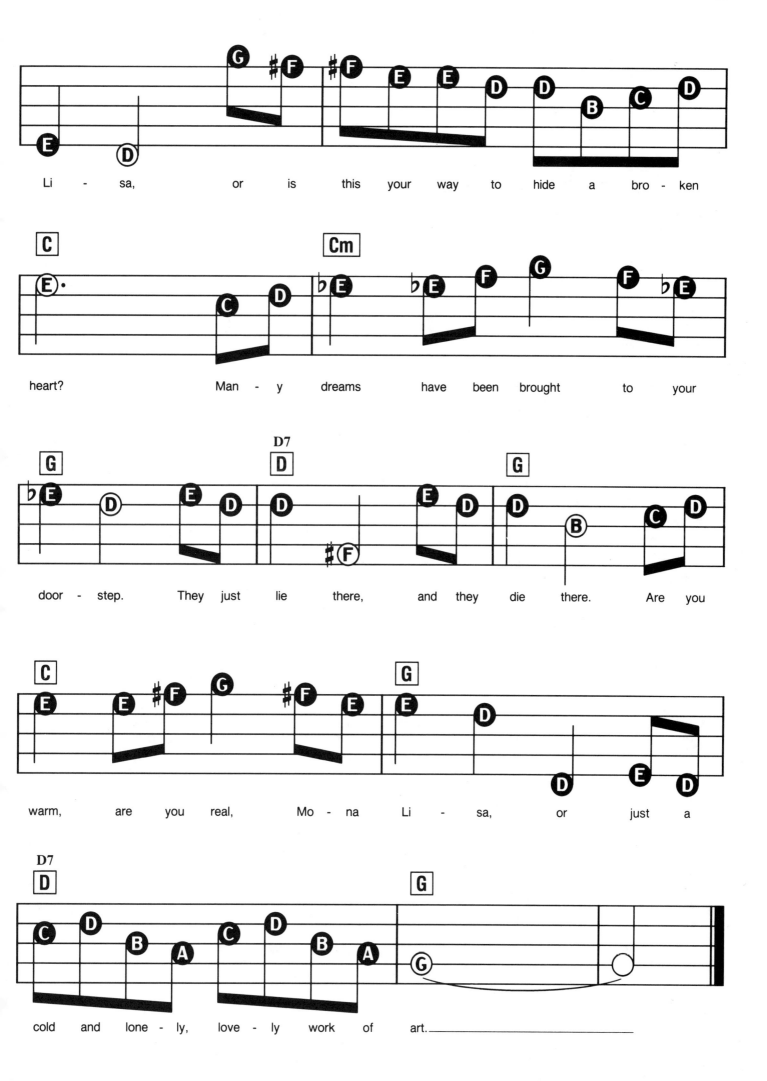

My Favorite Things
(From "THE SOUND OF MUSIC")

Registration 9
Rhythm: Waltz

Lyrics by Oscar Hammerstein II
Music by Richard Rodgers

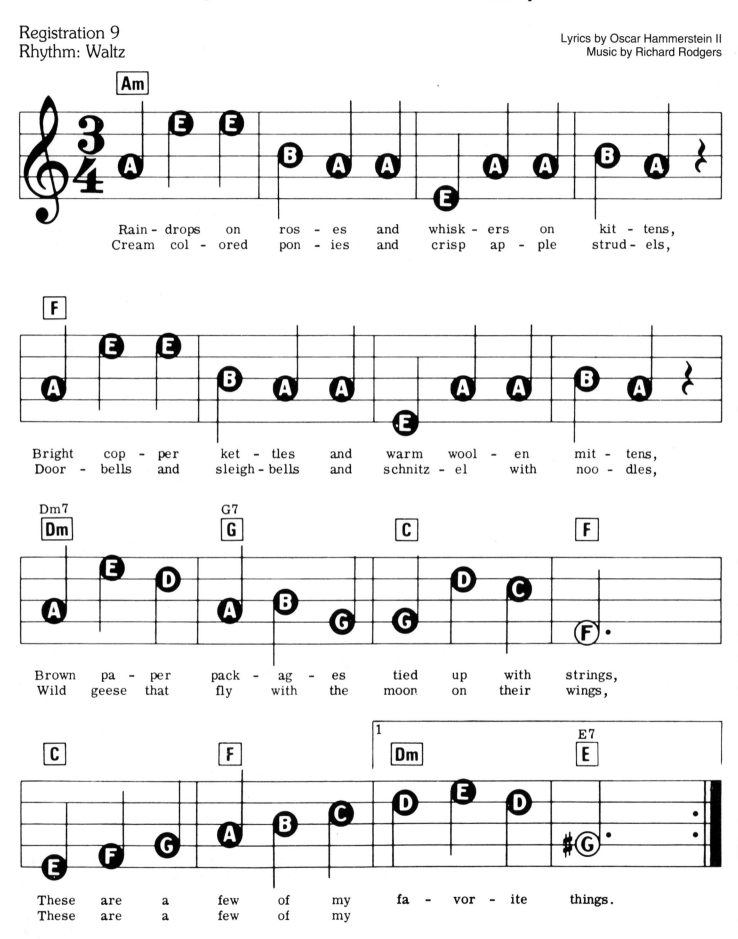

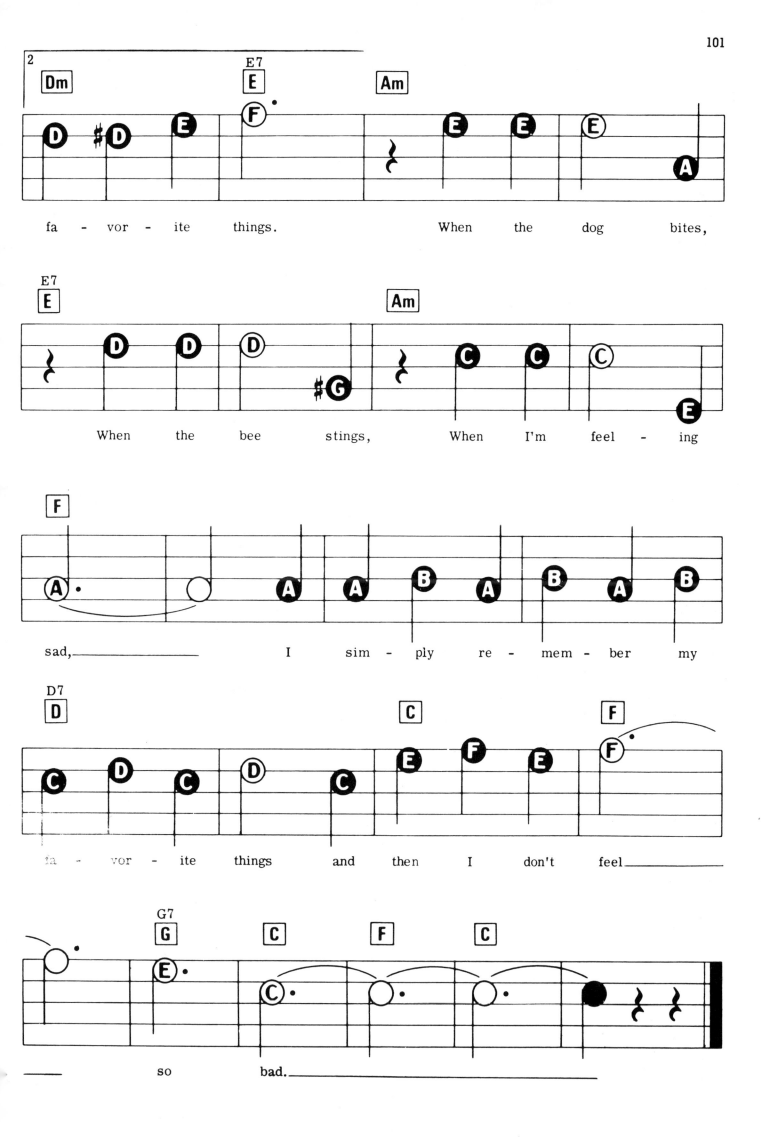

P.S. I Love You

Registration 2
Rhythm: Swing or Fox Trot

Words by Johnny Mercer
Music by Gordon Jenkins

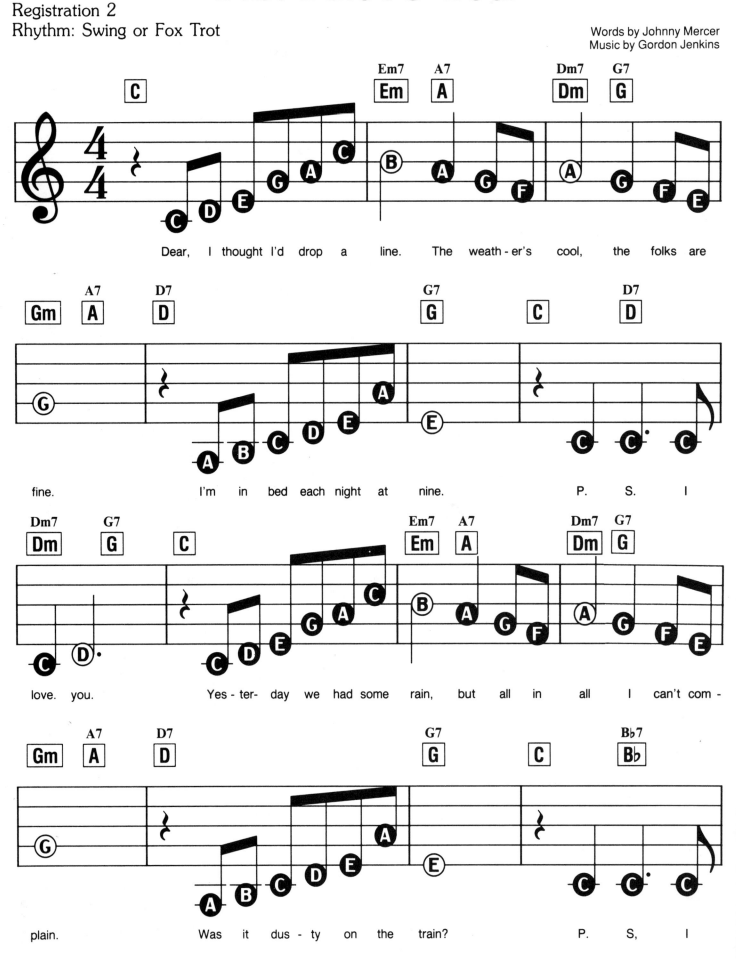

MCA music publishing

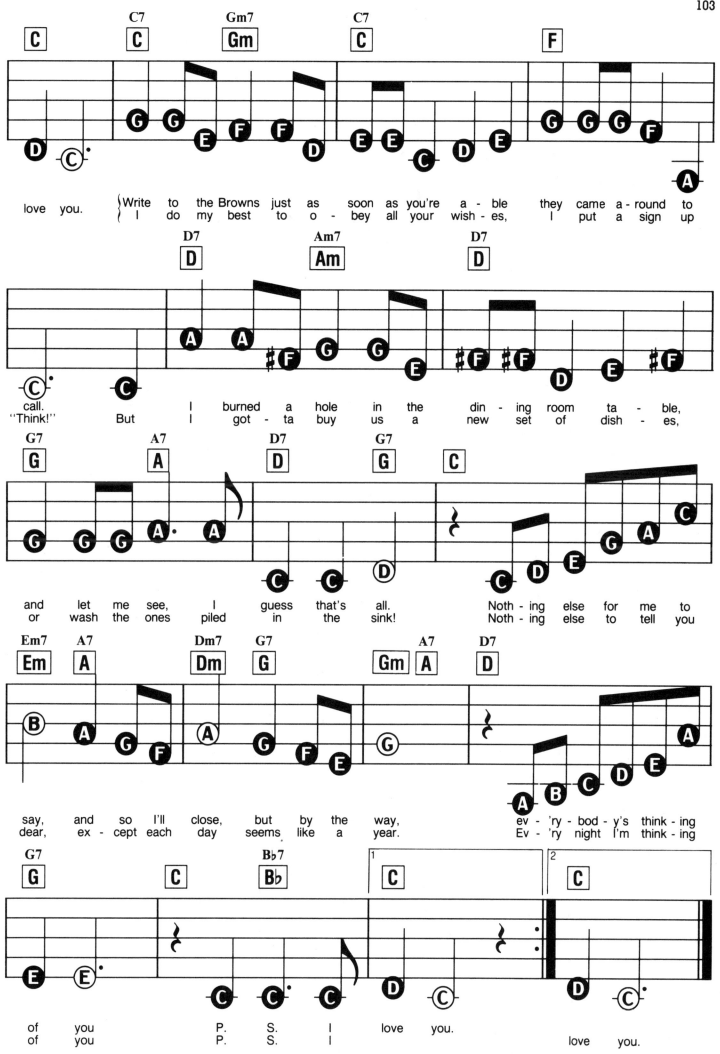

Secret Love

Registration 9
Rhythm: Swing

Lyric by Paul Francis Webster
Music by Sammy Fain

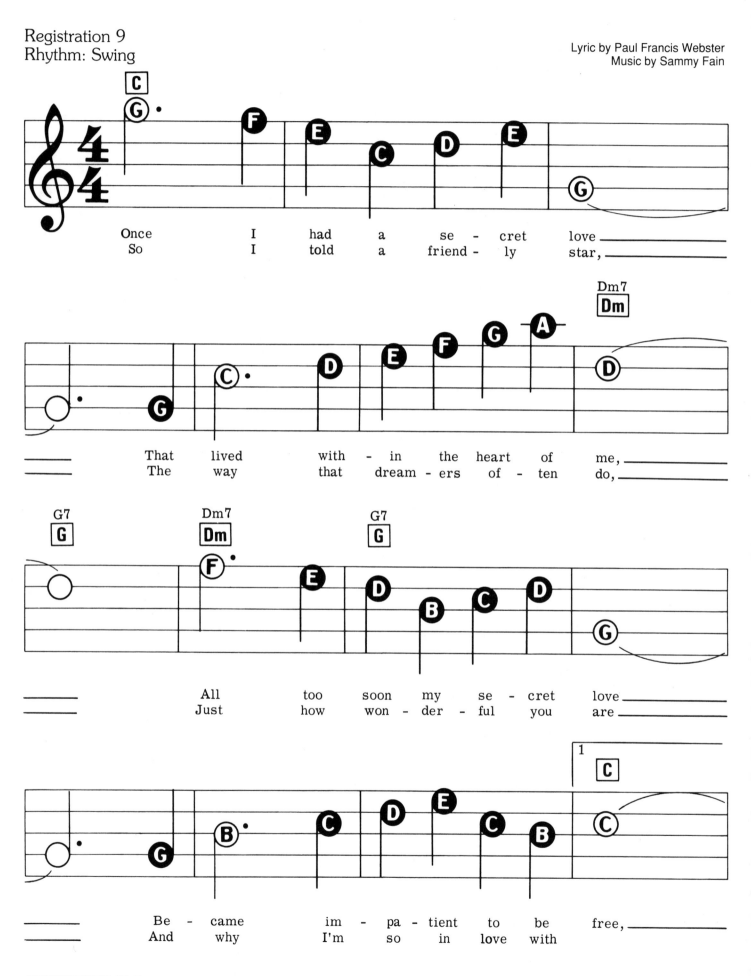

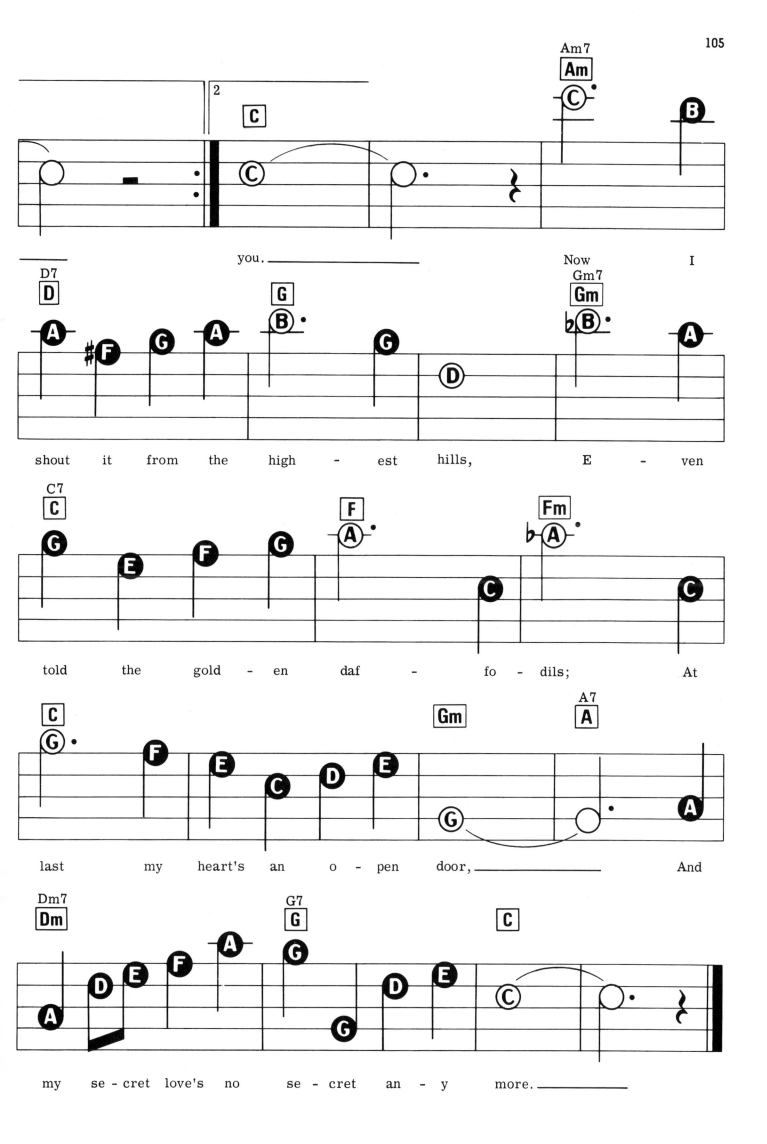

Shrimp Boats

Registration 4
Rhythm: Waltz

Words and Music by Paul Howard
and Paul Weston

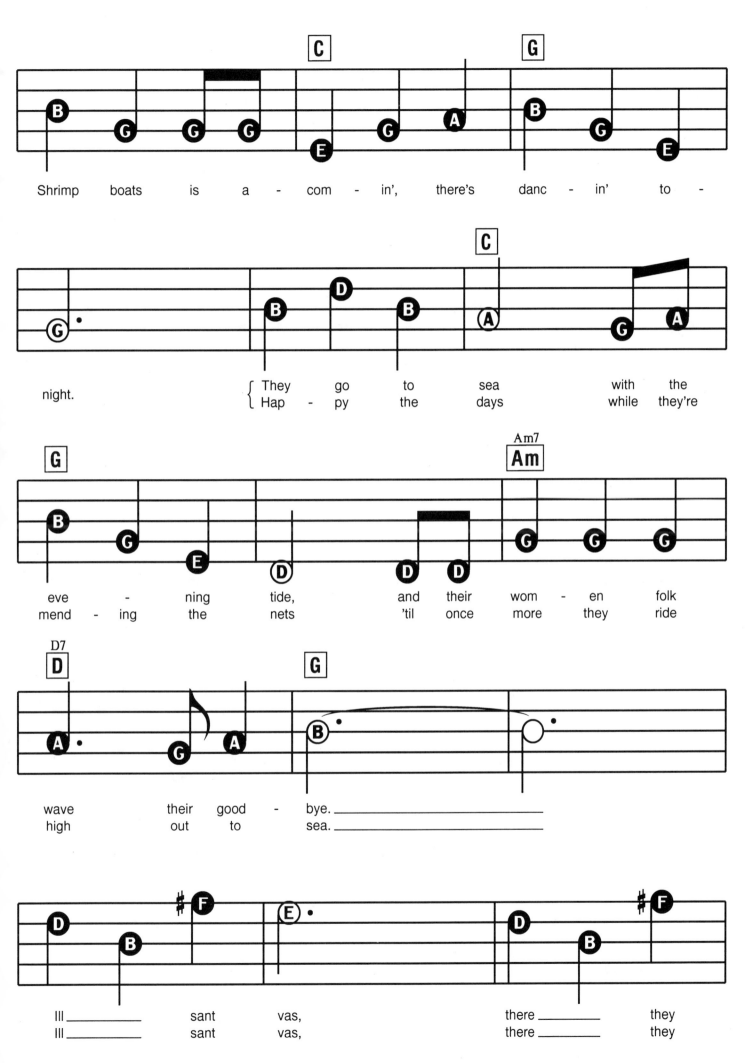

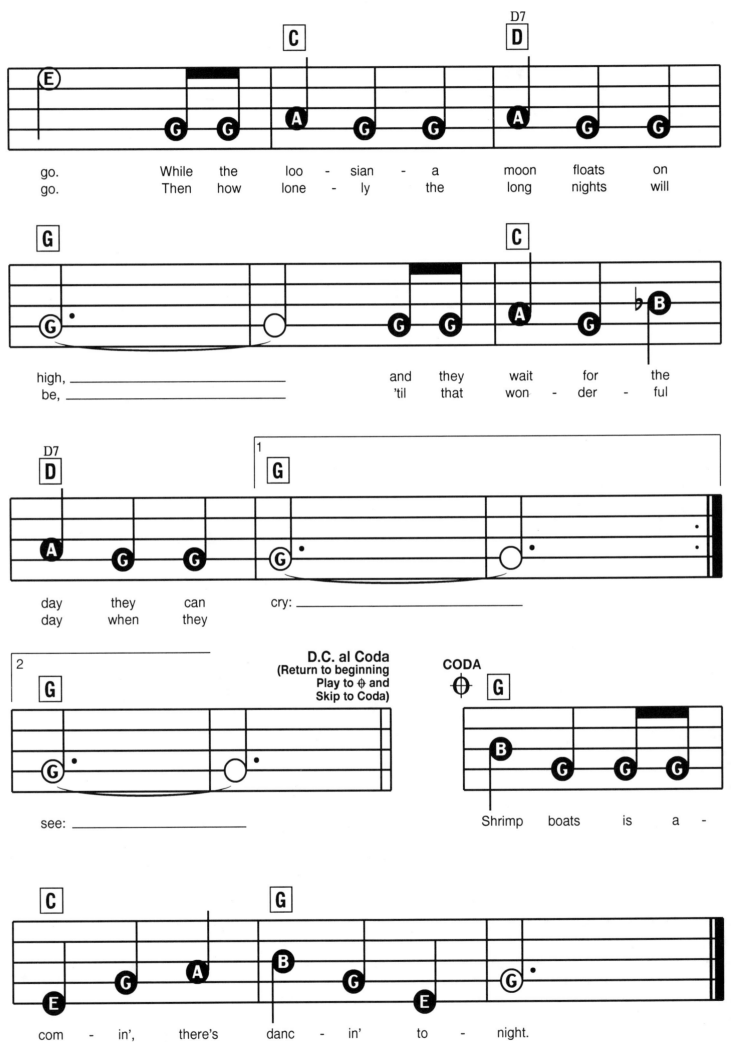

Small World
(From "GYPSY")

Registration 9
Rhythm: Fox Trot or Swing

Words by Stephen Sondheim
Music by Jule Styne

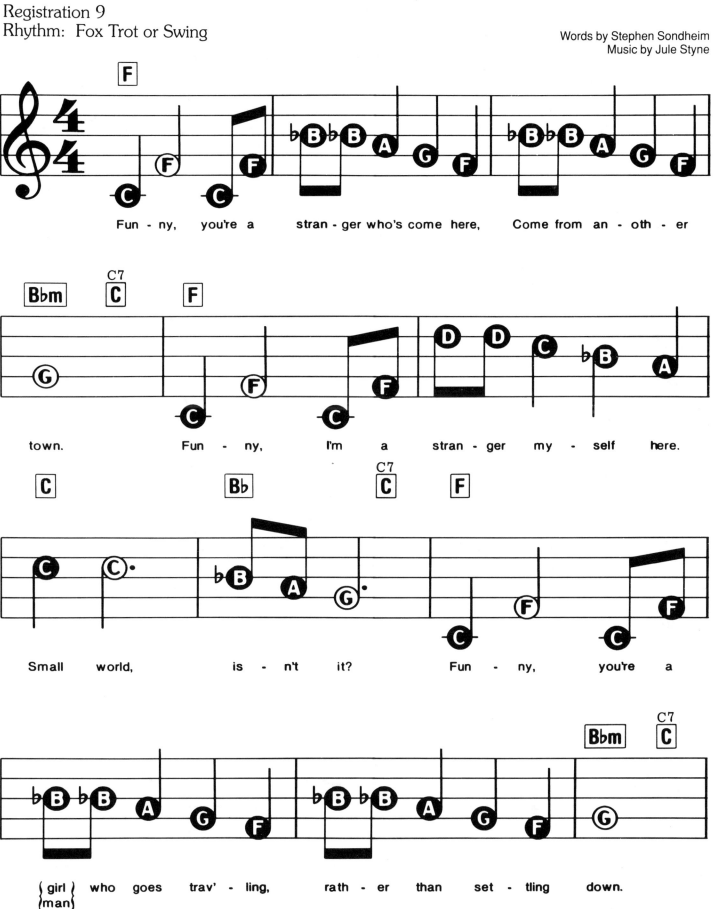

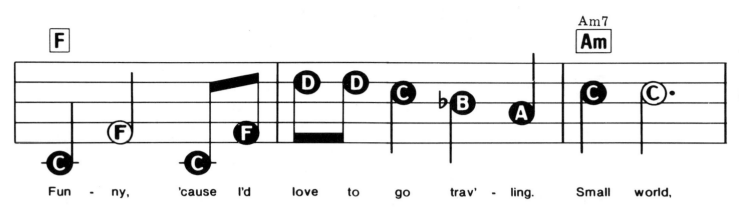

Fun - ny, 'cause I'd love to go trav' - ling. Small world,

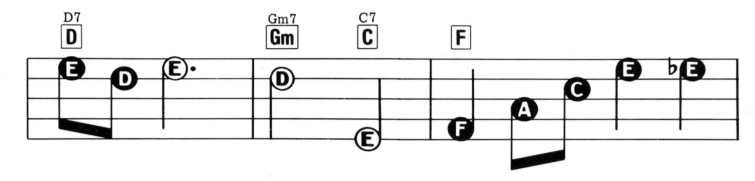

is - n't it? We have so much in com - mon

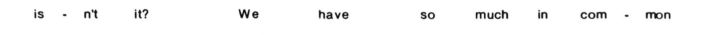
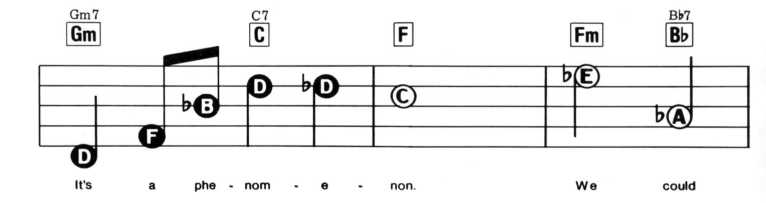

It's a phe - nom - e - non. We could

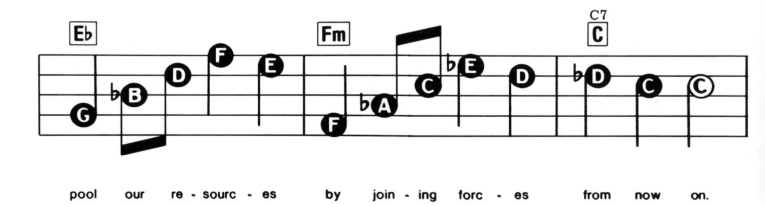

pool our re - sourc - es by join - ing forc - es from now on.

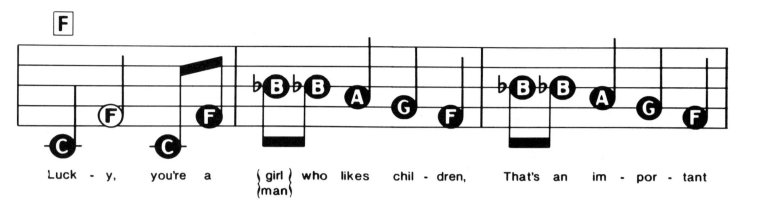

Luck - y, you're a {girl}{man} who likes chil - dren, That's an im - por - tant

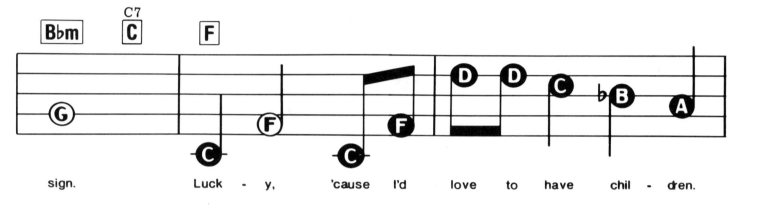

sign. Luck - y, 'cause I'd love to have chil - dren.

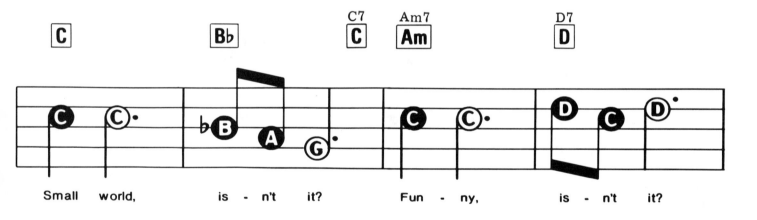

Small world, is - n't it? Fun - ny, is - n't it?

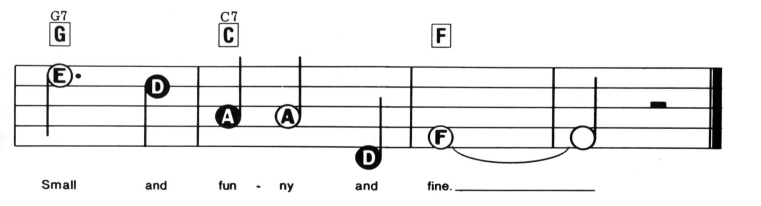

Small and fun - ny and fine. _____

Silver Bells
(From The Paramount Picture "THE LEMON DROP KID")

Registration 7
Rhythm: Waltz

Words and Music by Jay Livingston
and Ray Evans

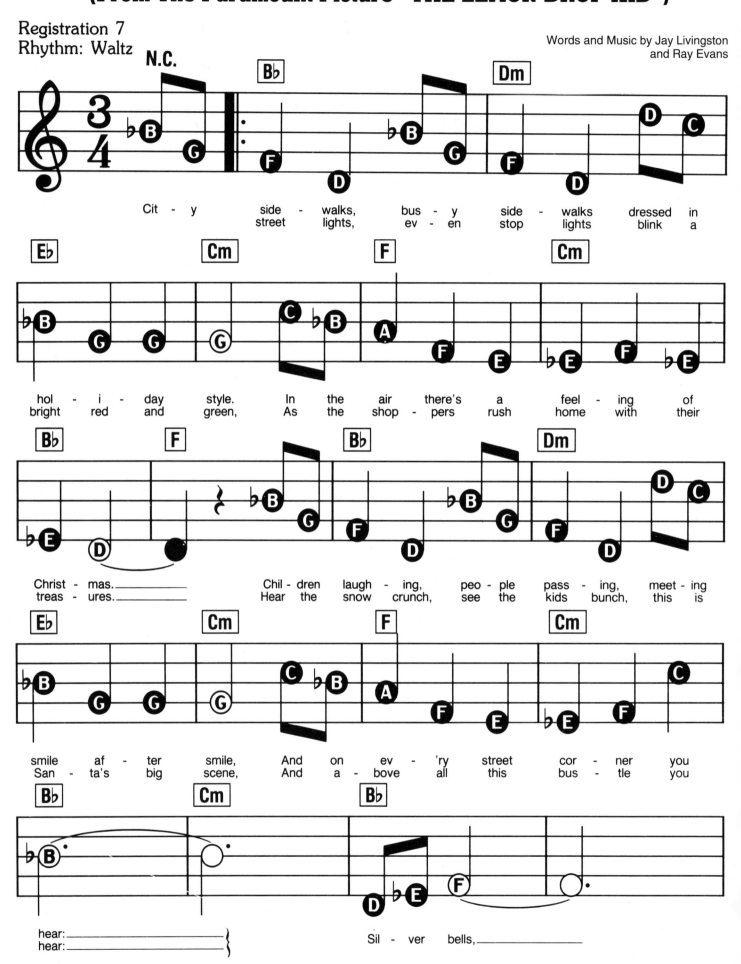

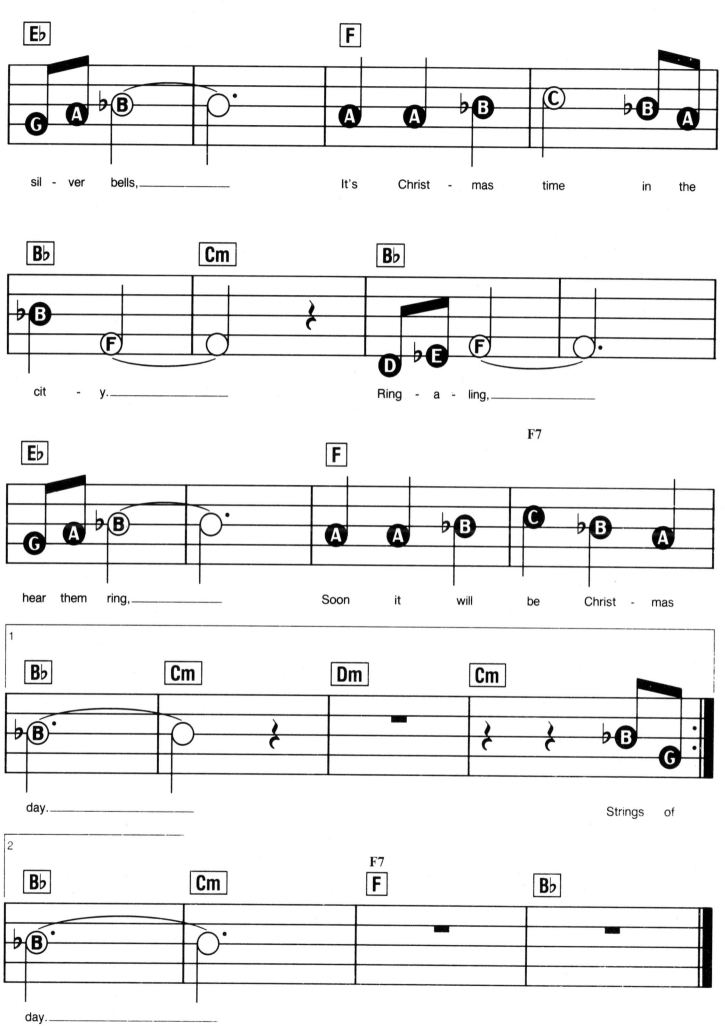

Wouldn't It Be Loverly
from MY FAIR LADY

Registration 5
Rhythm: Fox Trot

Words by Alan Jay Lerner
Music by Frederick Loewe

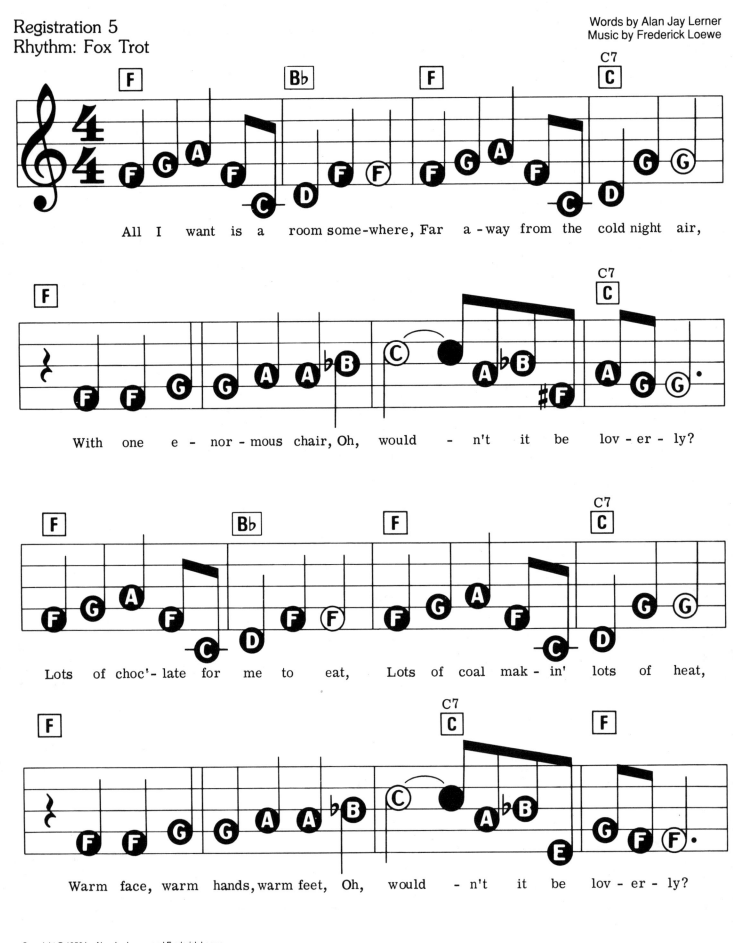

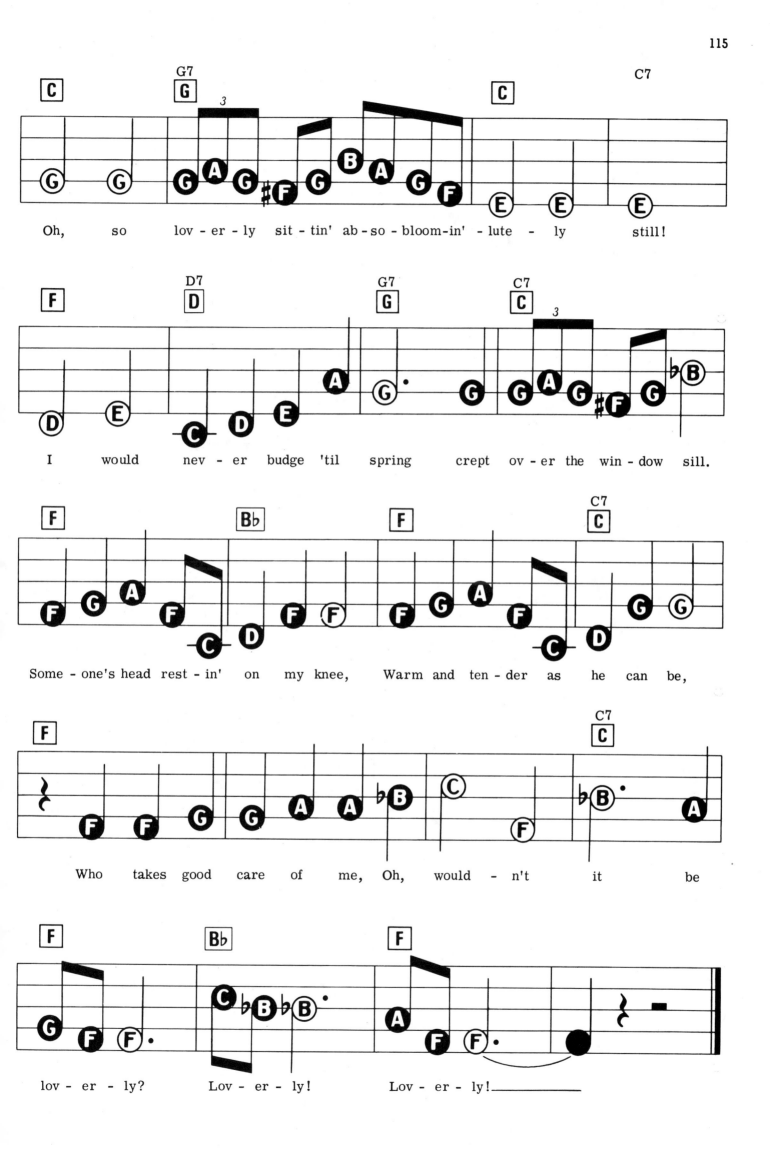

(Let Me Be Your) Teddy Bear

Registration 1
Rhythm: Rock

Words and Music by Kal Mann
and Bernie Lowe

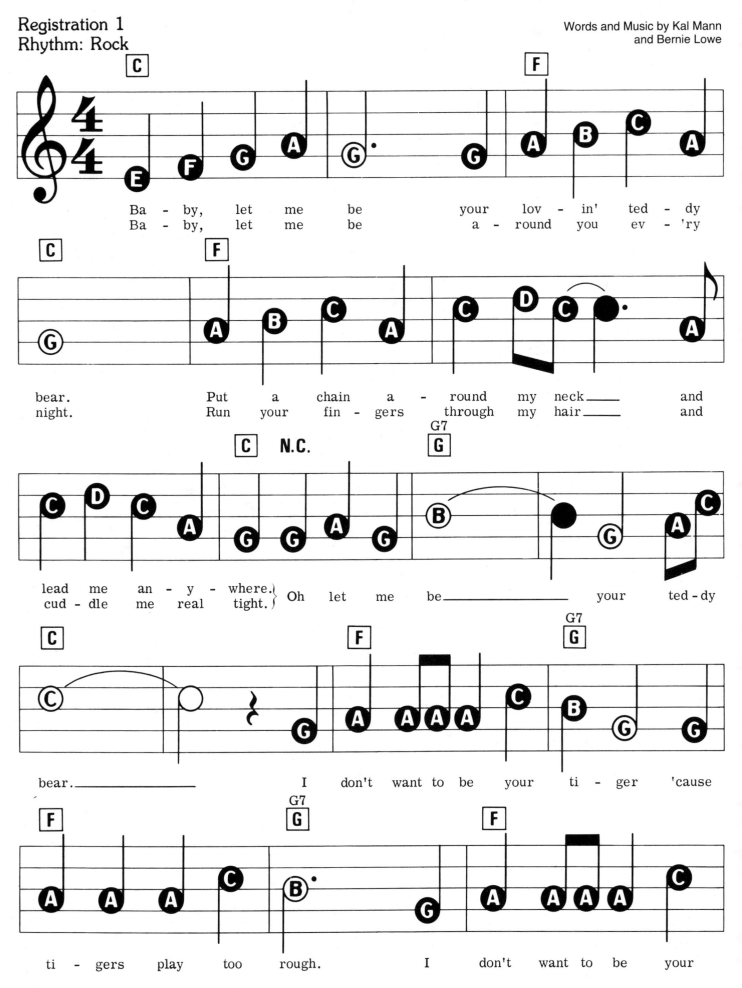

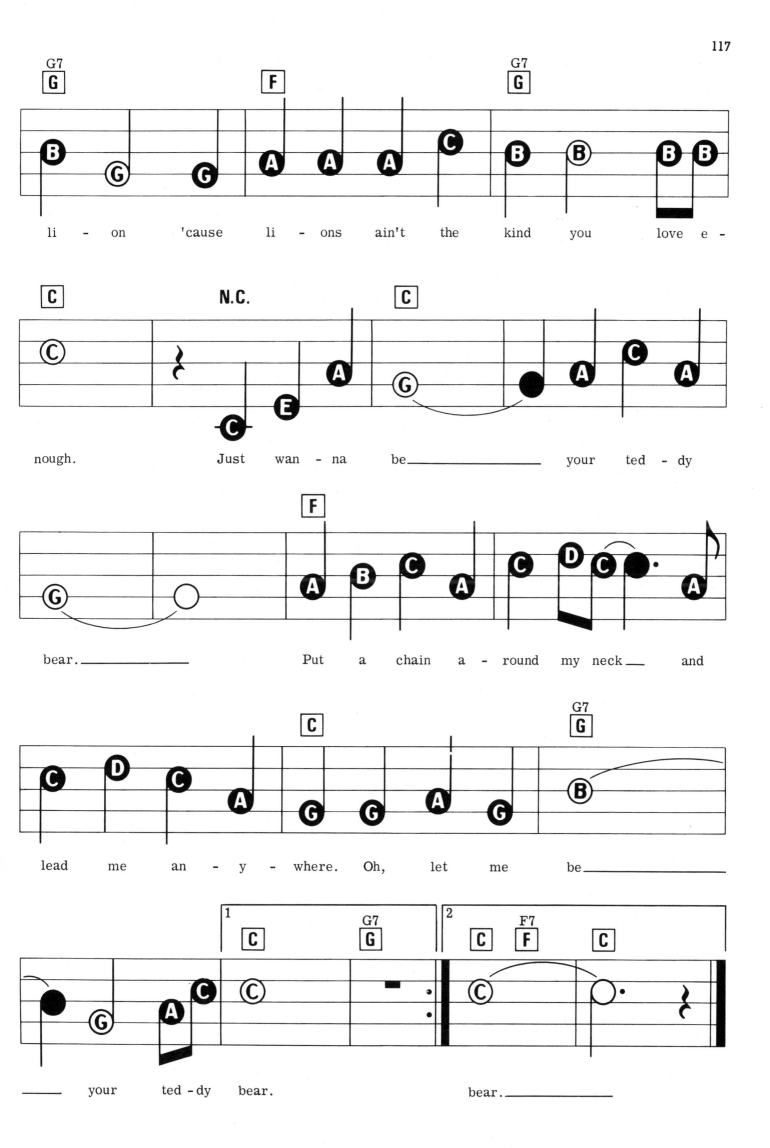

That's Amoré
(That's Love)
(From The Paramount Picture "THE CADDY")

Registration 3
Rhythm: Waltz

Words by Jack Brooks
Music by Harry Warren

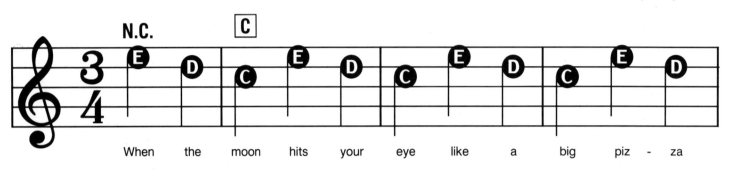

When the moon hits your eye like a big piz - za

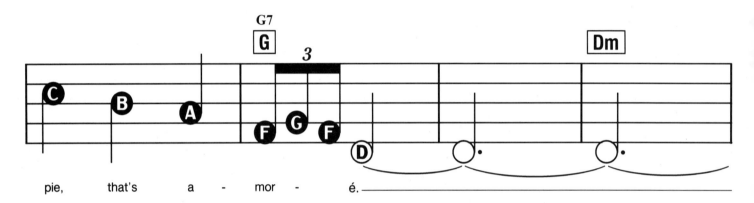

pie, that's a - mor - é. _____

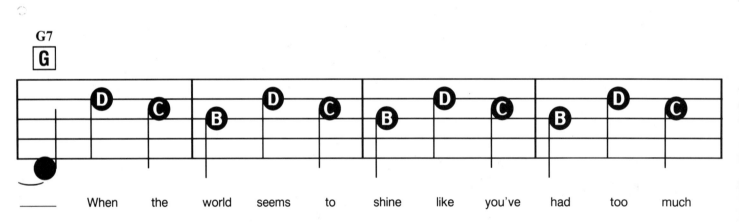

_____ When the world seems to shine like you've had too much

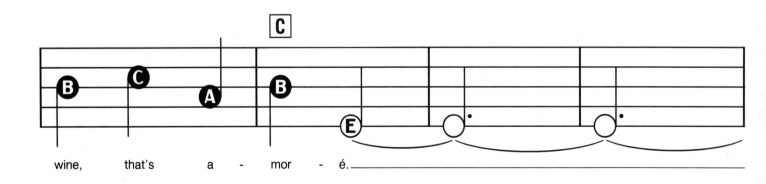

wine, that's a - mor - é. _____

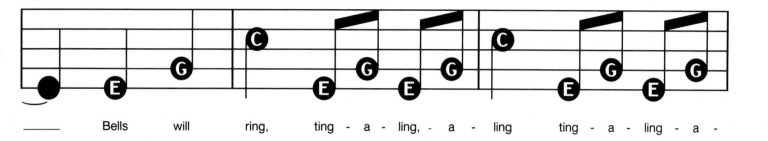

Bells will ring, ting - a - ling, - a - ling ting - a - ling - a -

G7

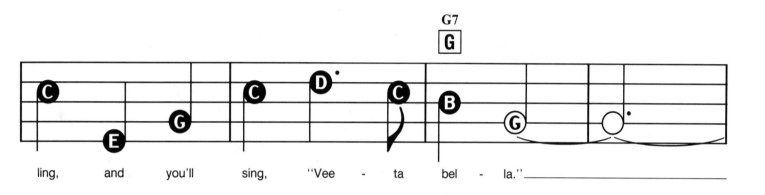

ling, and you'll sing, "Vee - ta bel - la." _____

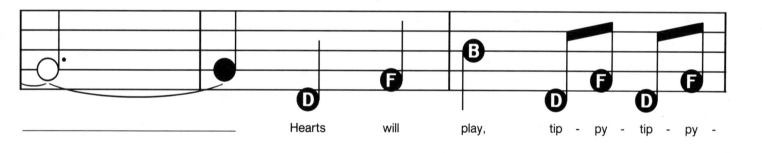

_____ Hearts will play, tip - py - tip - py -

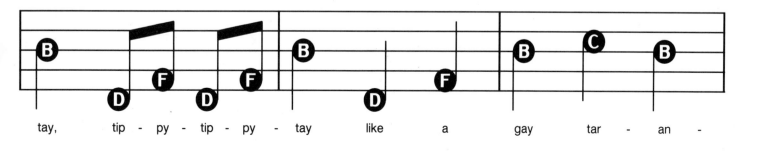

tay, tip - py - tip - py - tay like a gay tar - an -

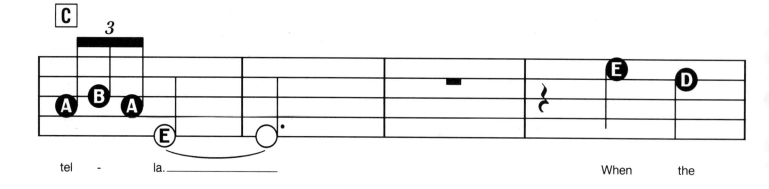

tel - la._____ When the

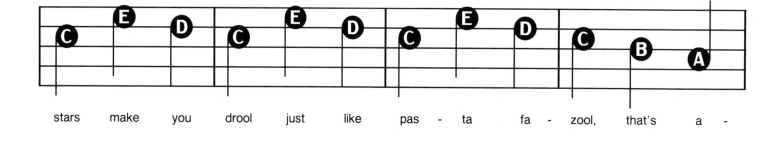

stars make you drool just like pas - ta fa - zool, that's a -

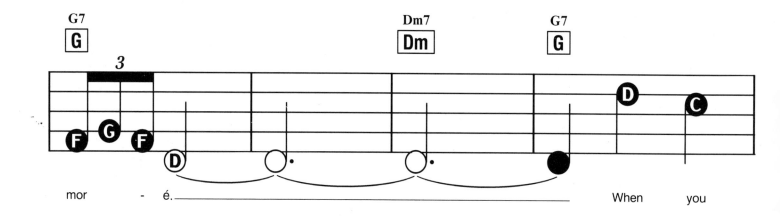

mor - é._____ When you

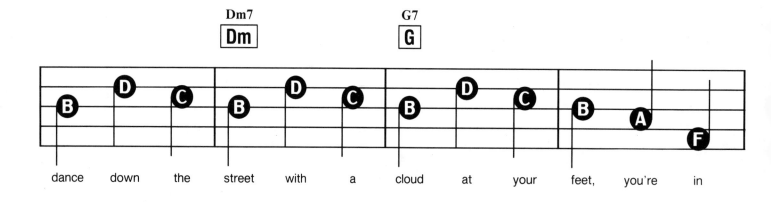

dance down the street with a cloud at your feet, you're in

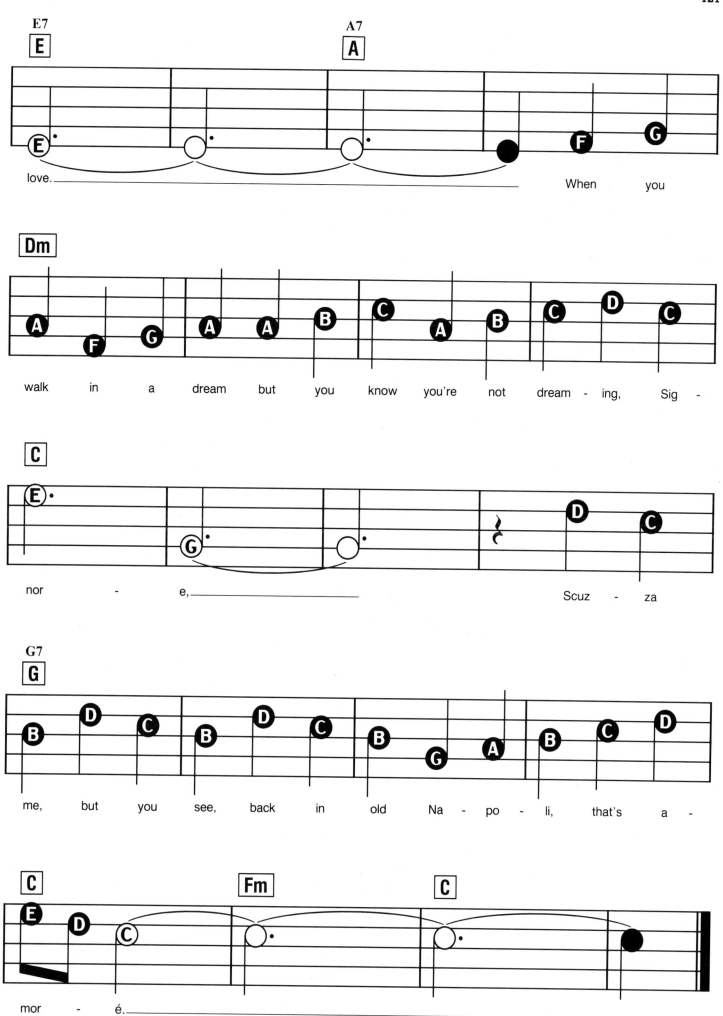

That's Entertainment
(From "THE BAND WAGON")

Registration 5
Rhythm: Fox Trot or Swing

Words by Howard Dietz
Music by Arthur Schwartz

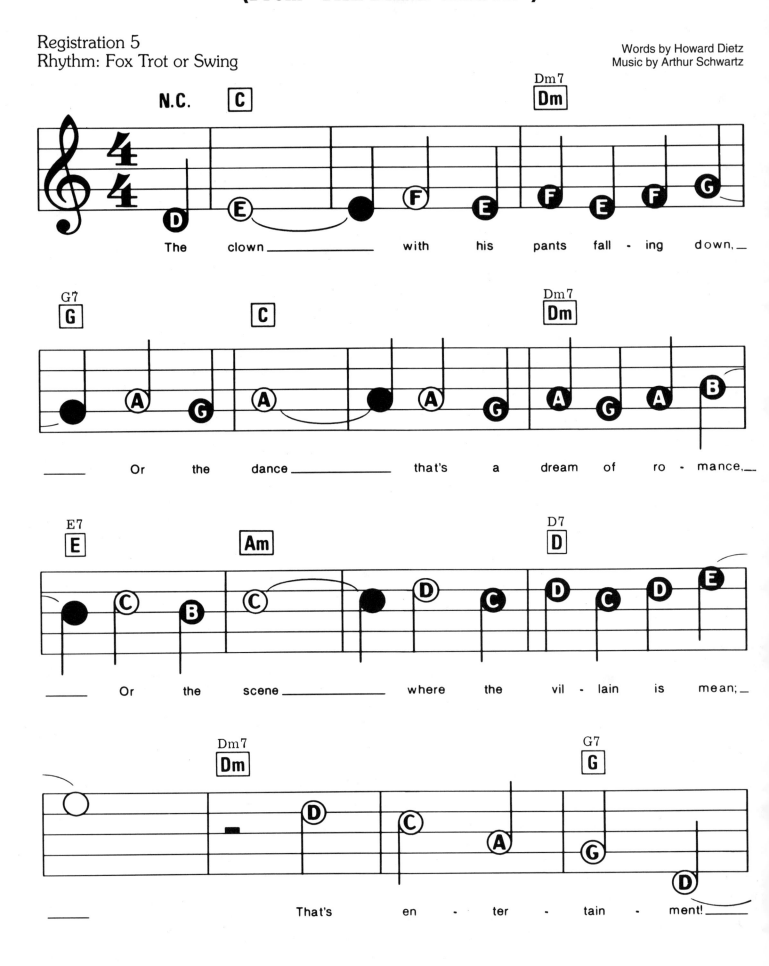

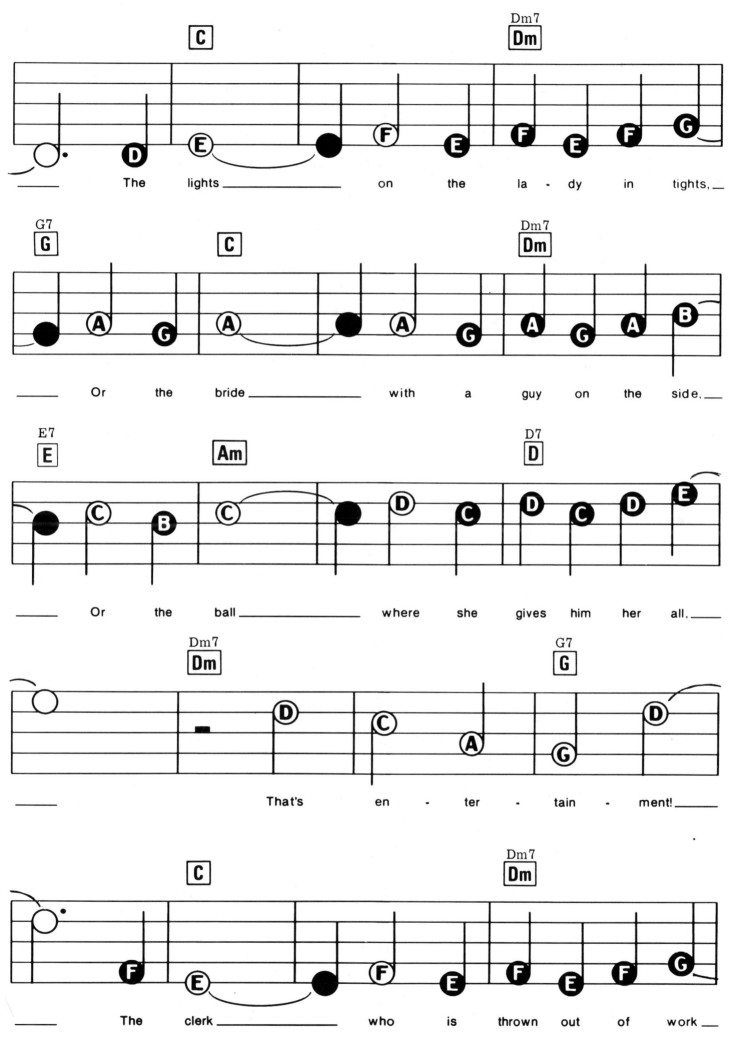

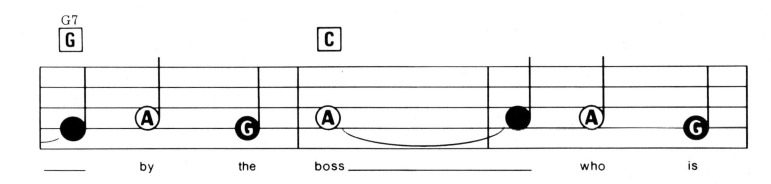

_____ by the boss _____ who is

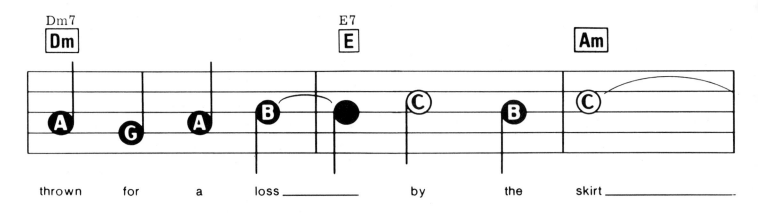

thrown for a loss _____ by the skirt _____

_____ who is do - ing him dirt; _____ The

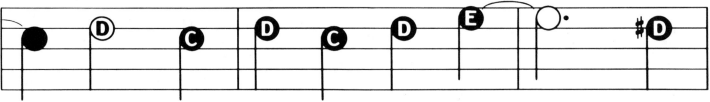

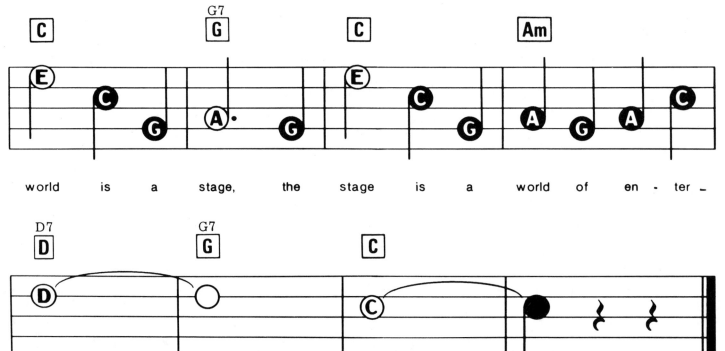

world is a stage, the stage is a world of en - ter _

tain - ment! _____

Too Much

Registration 4
Rhythm: Rock

Words and Music by Lee Rosenberg
and Bernie Weinman

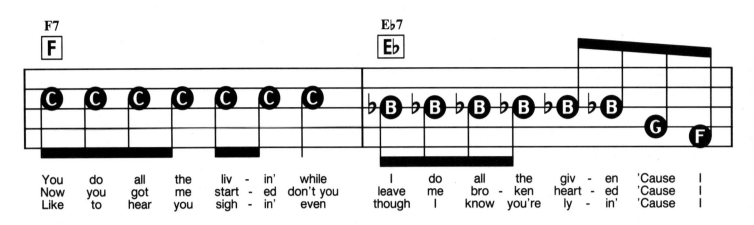

You do all the liv - in' while I do all the giv - en 'Cause I
Now you got me start - ed don't you leave me bro - ken heart - ed 'Cause I
Like to hear you sigh - in' even though I know you're ly - in' 'Cause I

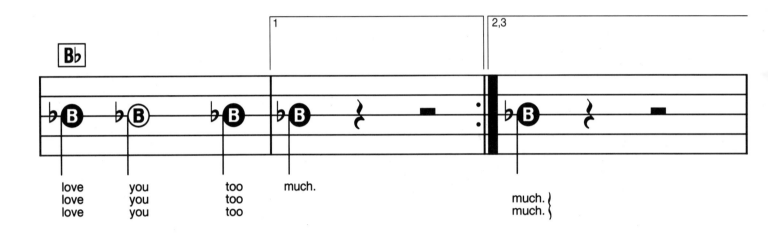

love you too much.
love you too much.
love you too much.

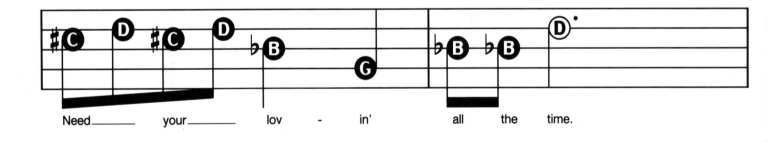

Need_____ your_____ lov - in' all the time.

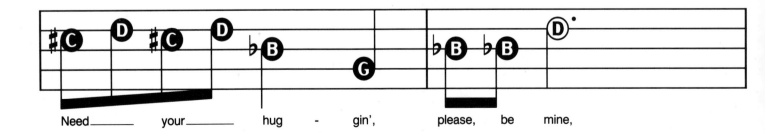

Need_____ your_____ hug - gin', please, be mine,

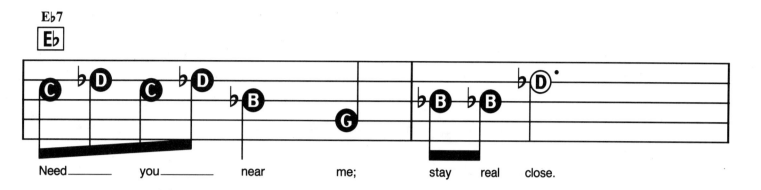

Eb7

Eb

Need_____ you_____ near me; stay real close.

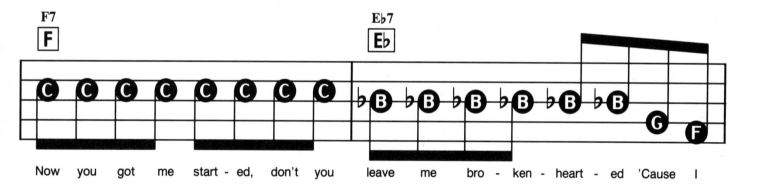

Bb

Please,_____ please,_____ hear me, you're the most.

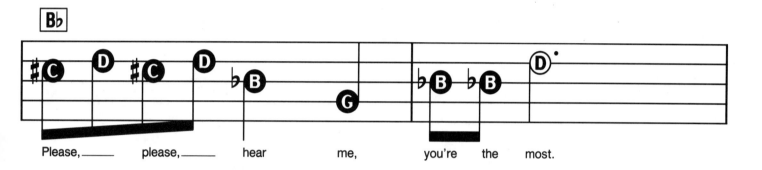

F7

F

Now you got me start - ed, don't you leave me bro - ken - heart - ed 'Cause I

Eb7

Eb

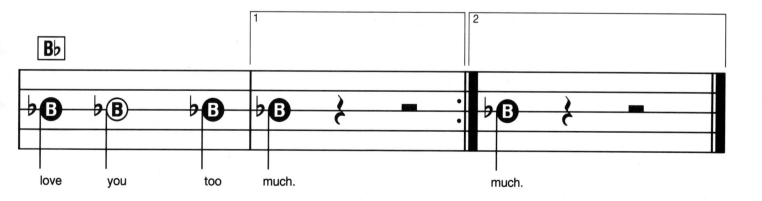

Bb

| 1 | 2 |

love you too much. much.

Till

Registration 2
Rhythm: Fox Trot or Ballad

Words by Carl Sigman
Music by Charles Danvers

129

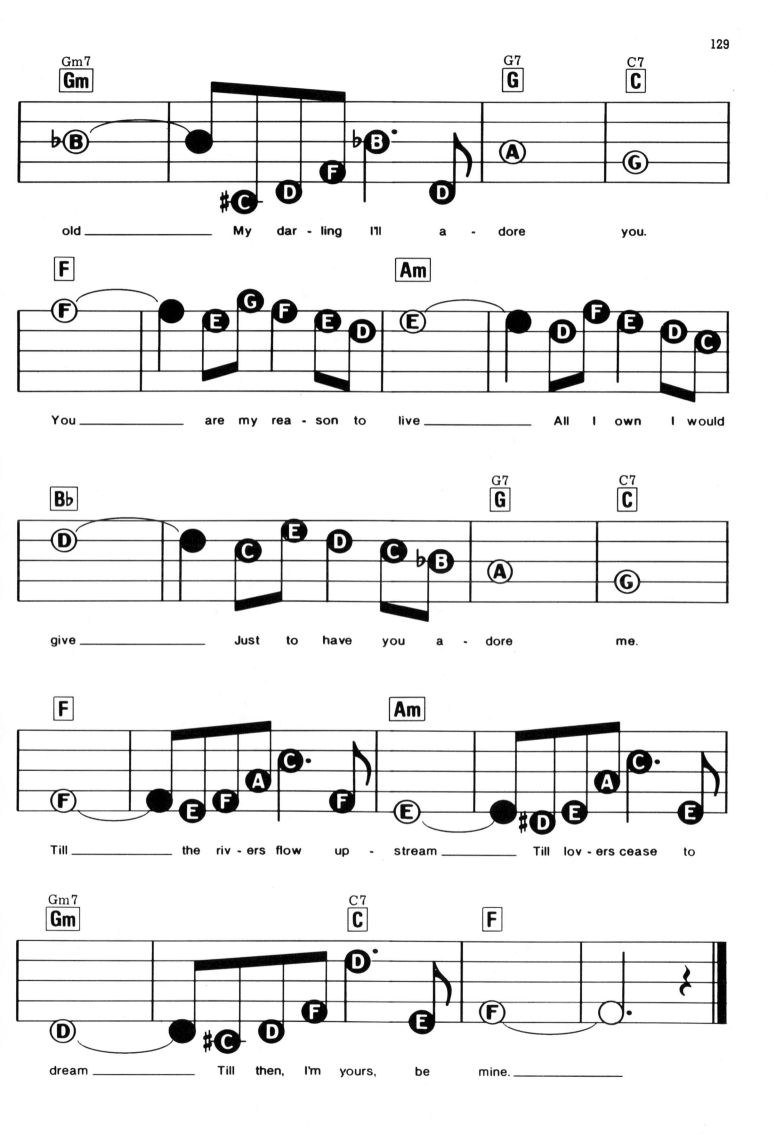

Tutti Frutti

Registration 4
Rhythm: Rock or 8 Beat

Words and Music by Richard Penniman
and D. La Bostrie

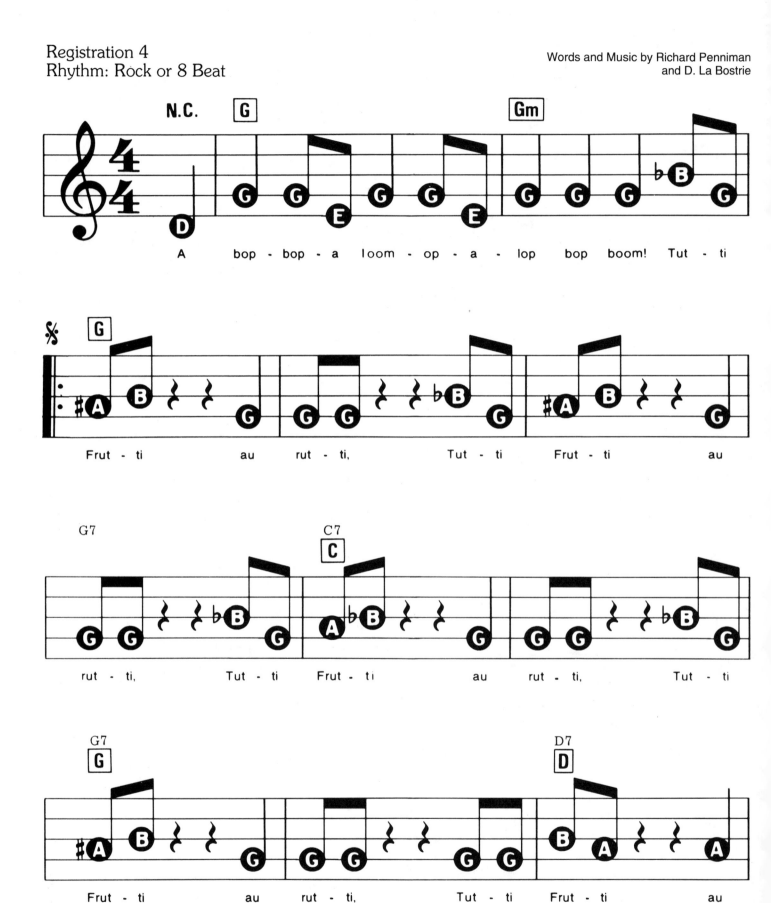

MCA music publishing

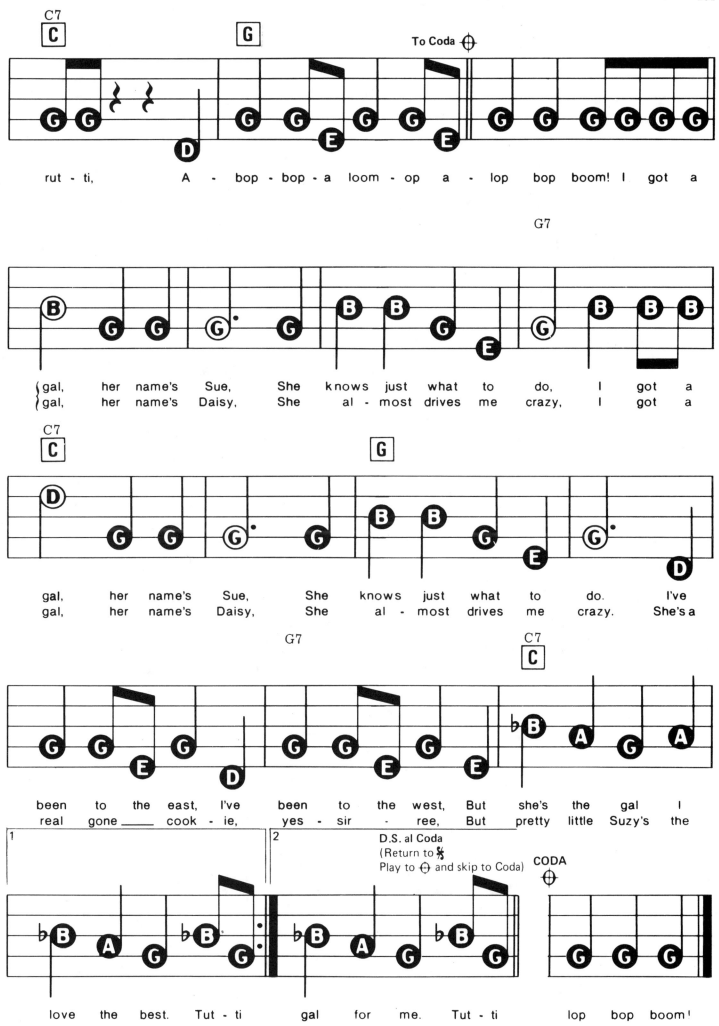

Wish You Were Here
(From "WISH YOU WERE HERE")

Registration 5
Rhythm: Beguine or Latin

Words and Music by
Harold Rome

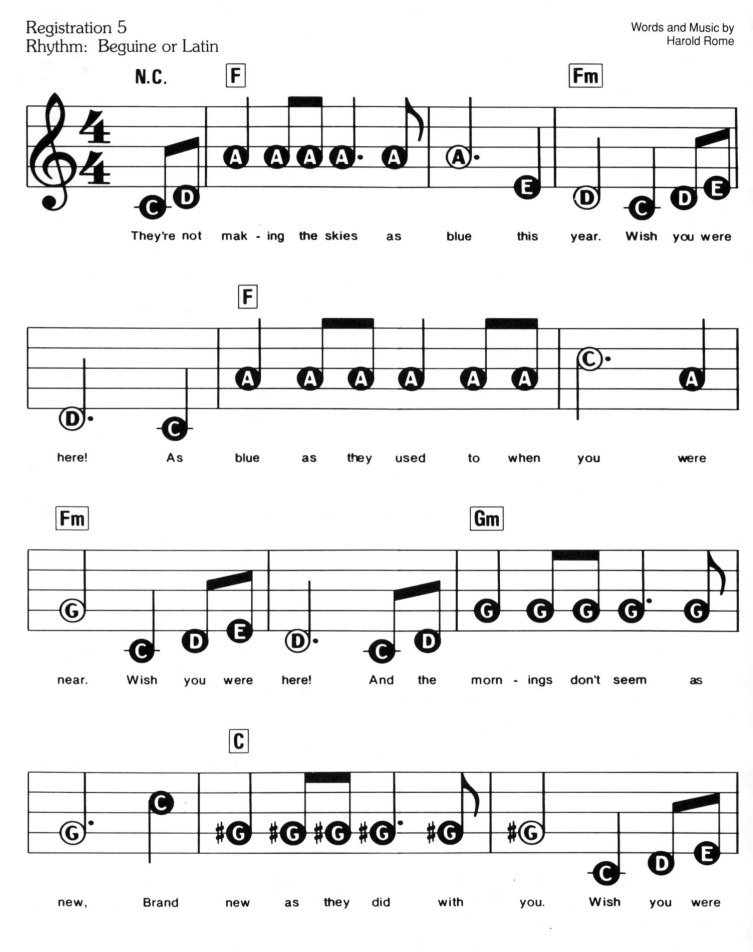

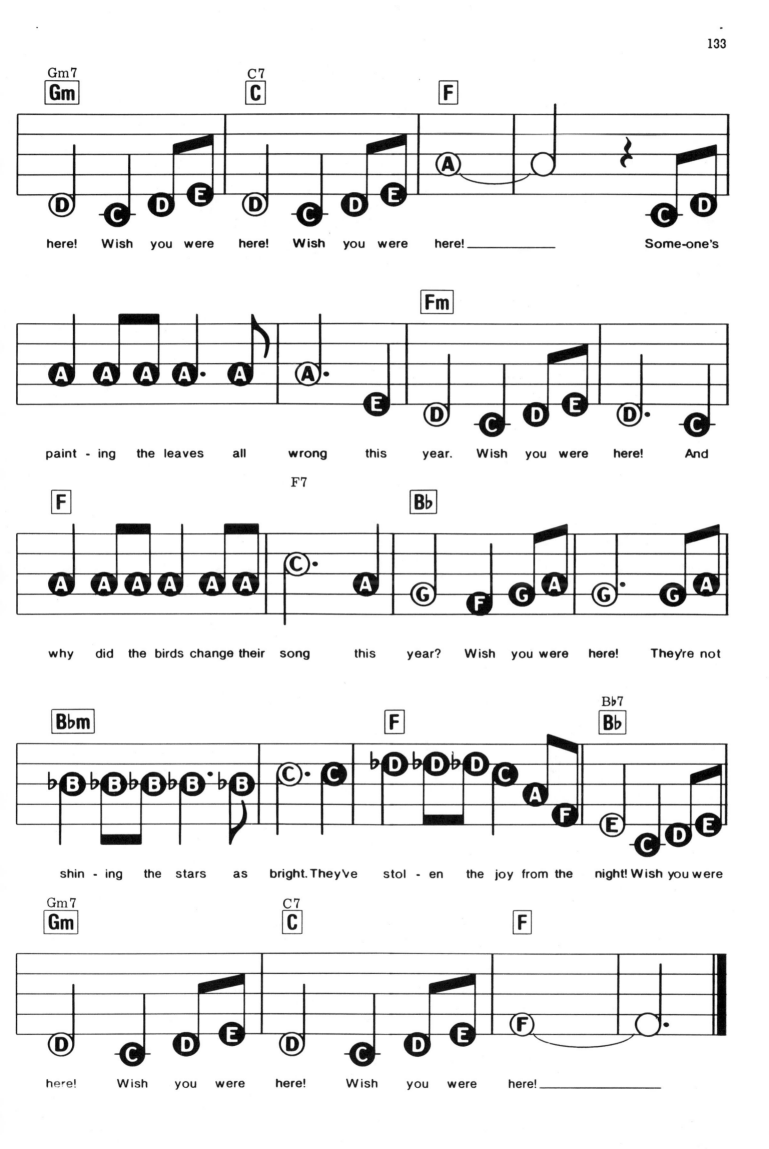

Yakety Yak

Registration 10
Rhythm: Rock

Words and Music by Jerry Leiber
and Mike Stoller

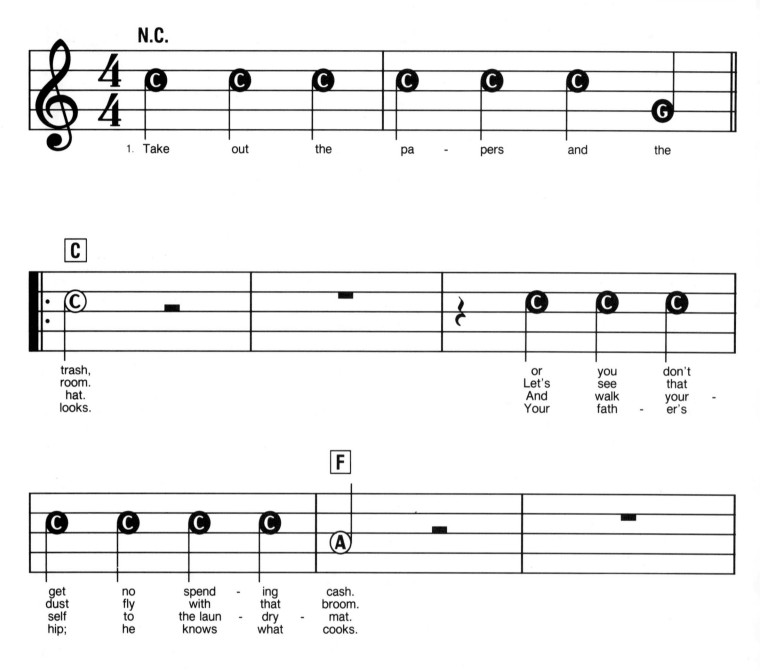

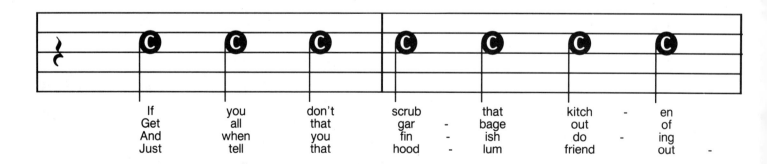

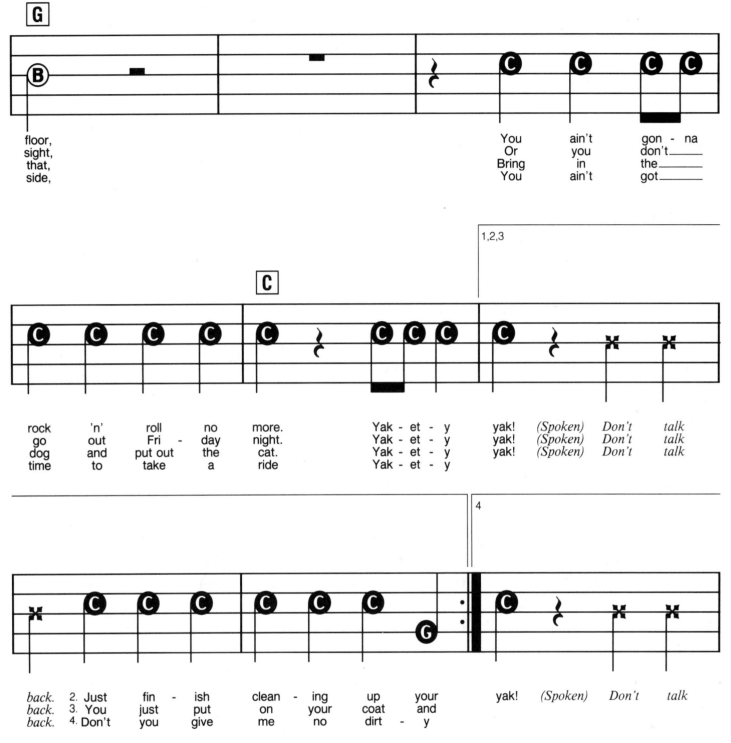

G7

floor,
sight,
that,
side,

You ain't gon - na
Or you don't_____
Bring in the_____
You ain't got_____

1,2,3

rock 'n' roll no more. Yak - et - y yak! *(Spoken) Don't talk*
go out Fri - day night. Yak - et - y yak! *(Spoken) Don't talk*
dog and put out the cat. Yak - et - y yak! *(Spoken) Don't talk*
time to take a ride Yak - et - y

4

back. 2. Just fin - ish clean - ing up your yak! *(Spoken) Don't talk*
back. 3. You just put on your coat and
back. 4. Don't you give me no dirt - y

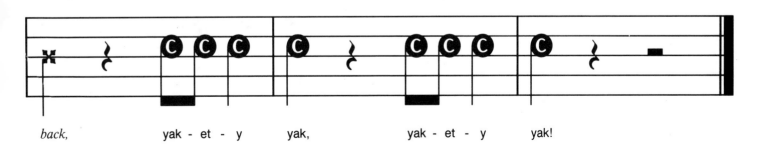

back, yak - et - y yak, yak - et - y yak!

(I Wonder Why?) You're Just In Love
(From The Stage Production "CALL ME MADAM")

Registration 2
Rhythm: Fox Trot or Ballad

Words and Music by
Irving Berlin

I hear sing- ing and there's no one there

—— I smell blos - soms and the

trees are bare_____ All day

long I seem to walk on air,_____ I won- der why?_____

137

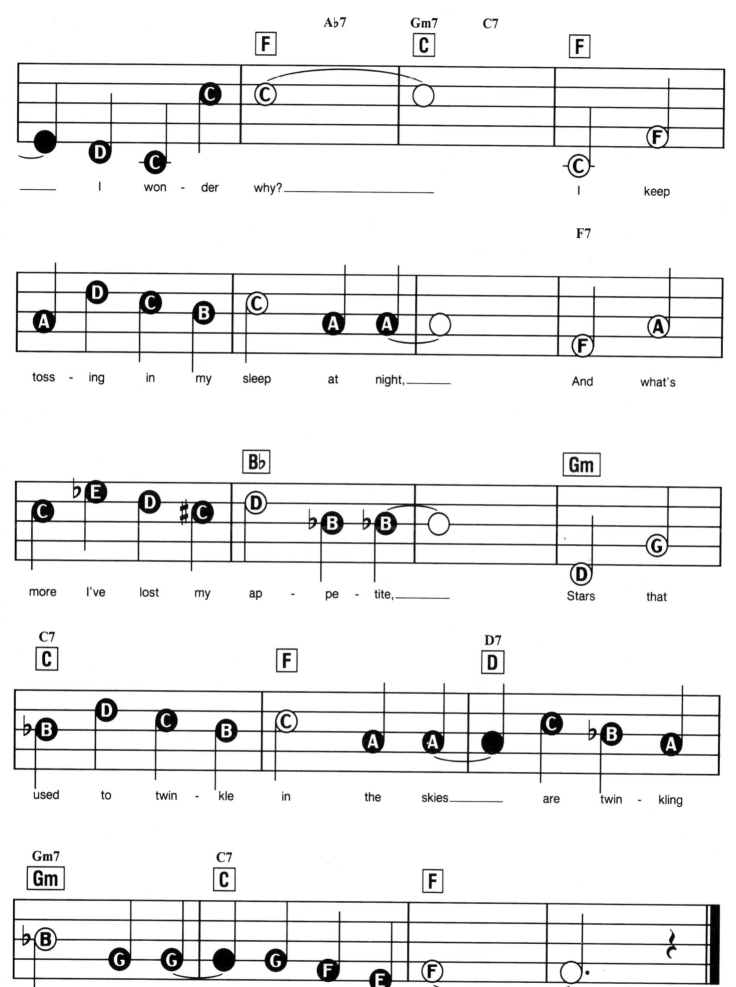

Young And Foolish
(From "PLAIN AND FANCY")

Registration 3
Rhythm: Fox Trot or Pops

Words by Arnold B. Horwitt
Music by Albert Hague

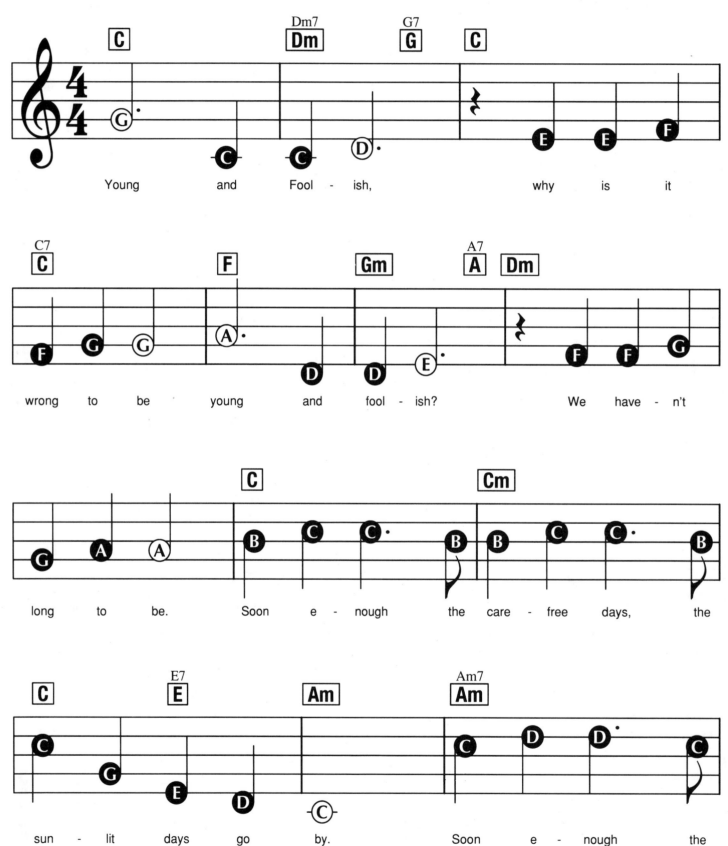

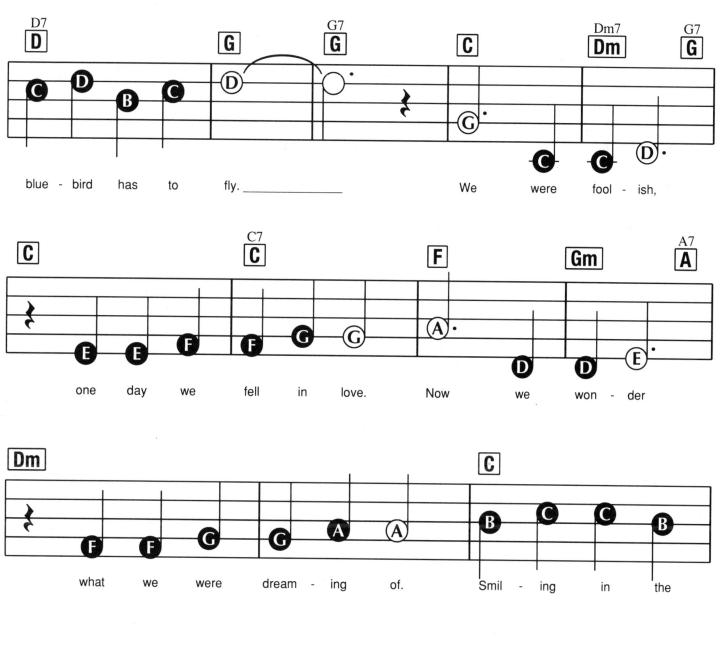

blue - bird   has   to   fly. _____   We   were   fool - ish,

one   day   we   fell   in   love.   Now   we   won - der

what   we   were   dream - ing   of.   Smil - ing   in   the

sun - light,   laugh - ing   in   the   rain.   I   wish   that   we   were

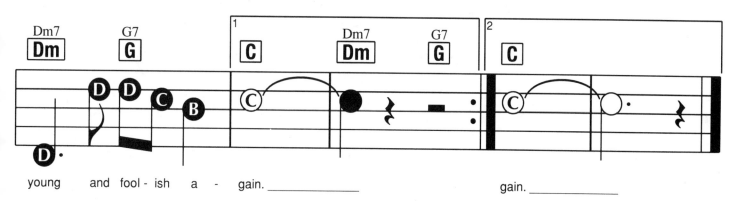

young   and   fool - ish a - gain. _____   gain. _____

Your Cheatin' Heart

Registration 5
Rhythm: Country Western or Ballad

Words and Music by
Hank Williams

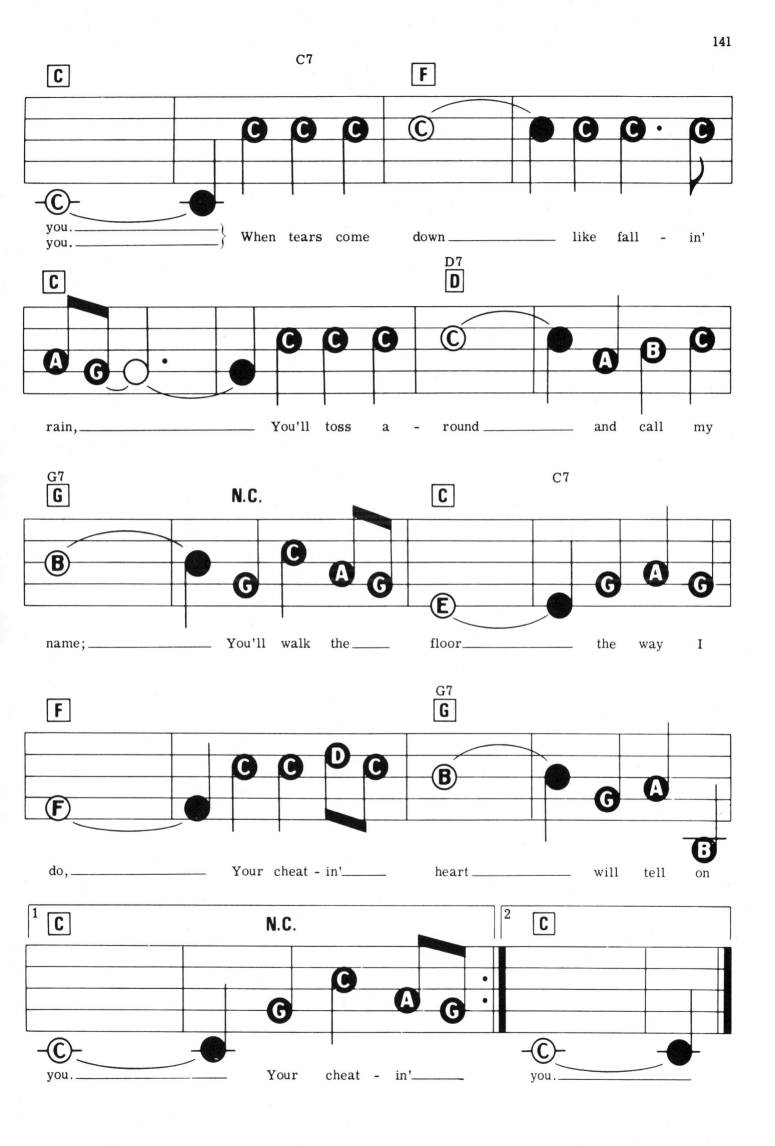

Why

Registration 7
Rhythm: Pops or Latin

Words and Music by Bob Marcucci
and Peter DeAngelis

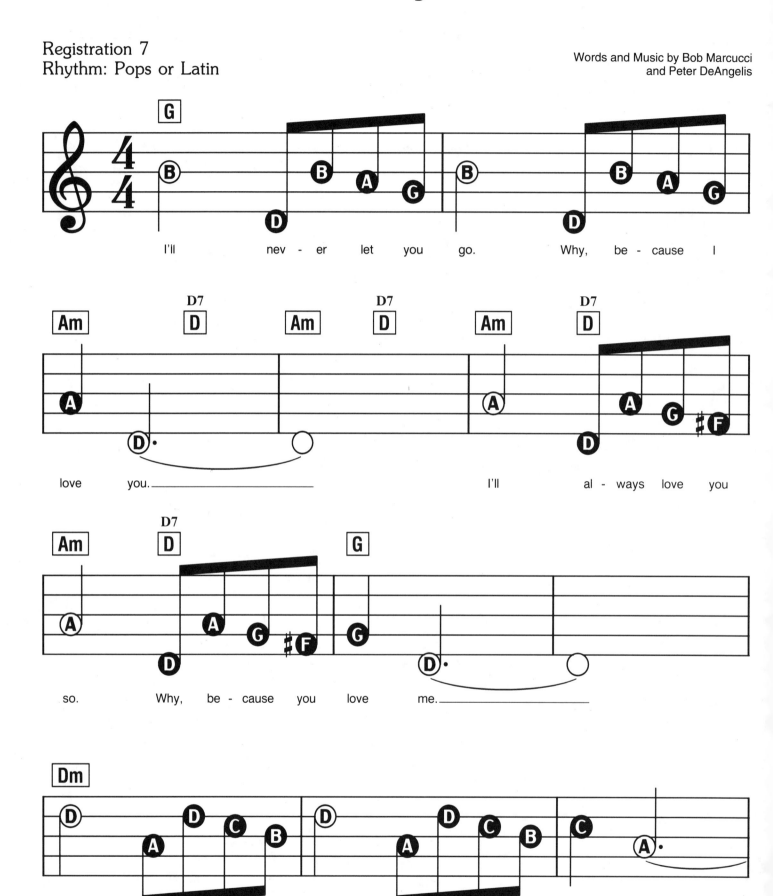

MCA music publishing

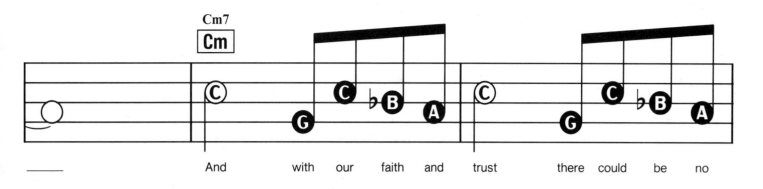

And with our faith and trust there could be no

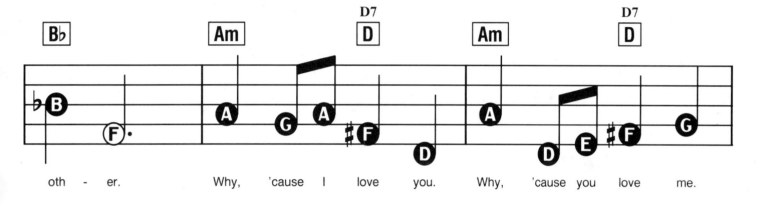

oth - er. Why, 'cause I love you. Why, 'cause you love me.

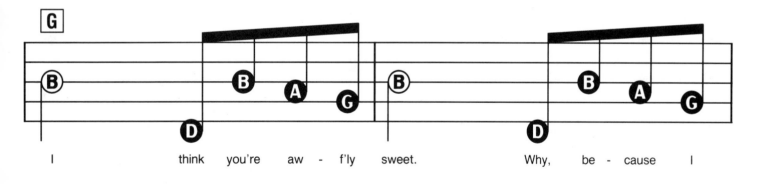

I think you're aw - f'ly sweet. Why, be - cause I

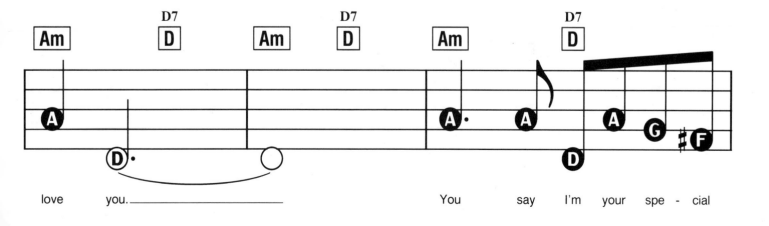

love you. You say I'm your spe - cial

144

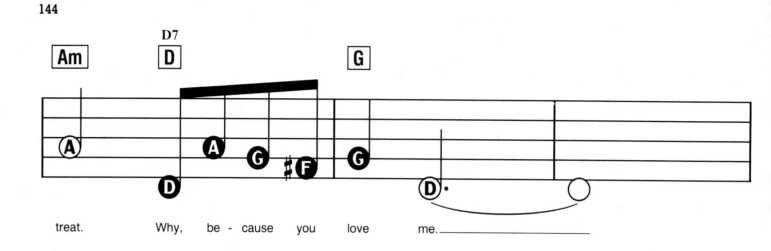

treat. Why, be - cause you love me._____

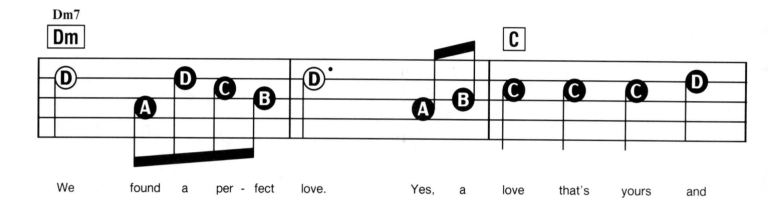

We found a per - fect love. Yes, a love that's yours and

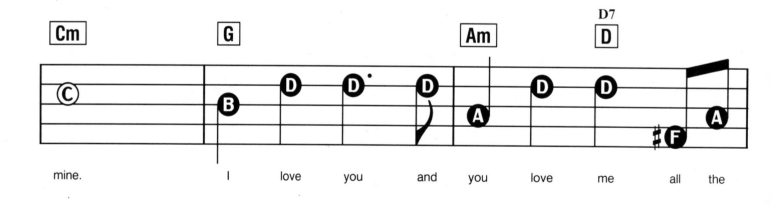

mine. I love you and you love me all the

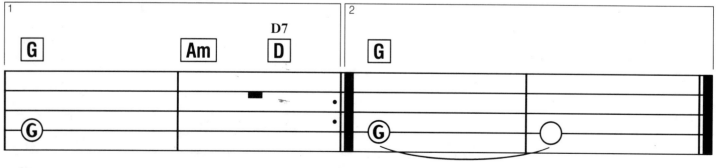

time. time._____